DECORATING YOUR COUNTRY PLACE

BY ELLEN LIMAN

The Money Saver's Guide
to Decorating
Decorating Your Country Place

DECORATING YOUR

COUNTRY PLACE

ELLEN LIMAN

Coward, McCann & Geoghegan, Inc.

New York

This book is dedicated to my mother and father

CONTENTS

DECORATING YOUR COUNTRY PLACE

Barns make popular vacation homes. This one, factory-built for on-site construction in New Hampshire, combines modern conveniences with the rustic charm of old-fashioned exposed posts and beams, walls of rough sawn plywood and pine floors. Large light bulbs on cords hang down at different levels from the peaked roof, and a carpet-covered hanging couch is not only fun but functional (it is easy to clean under).

INTRODUCTION

You've finally done it. You've closed title, traveled three hours, and taken possession. Now, what do you do when you discover that "furnished" means two squeaky beds and a caved-in couch and the painter tells you he's booked for a year in advance? Sell? No, buy this book.

You're not alone. Beginning with Thoreau, millions of others have joined the exodus to the country, seeking an escape from the pressures and pollution of the cities. Faster transportation, greater leisure, more money, the need for privacy and family togetherness, increased sensitivity to nature, and an urge to just plain "get away" have made owning a country place a goal even for people who live in suburban areas.

Whether an apartment at the beach, a cabin in the woods, a condominium on a golf course, or a ski house in the mountains, the common denominator of a country home is that it represents a change from one's normal environment. To some it will be change from a dark and confining apartment to the unbroken horizon and sunny skies of the beach or from urban noises to the stillness of a lake. To others, change can mean just the opposite, from the impersonal life of the city to the frenetic social life of a crowded resort community. Indeed, the very creative and experimental design of many country homes can be seen as a gesture of rebellion against the monotonous horizontal and vertical rectangles in which most of our urban and suburban population live. But whatever the architecture, it is the interior of the country home that will express its personality and set the tone for your leisure life-style. Face it, if you merely duplicate the decor of your permanent residence, you will hardly know you are away. Decorating the country home is a challenge unlike any other decorating experience: to furnish without benefit of department stores and professional help; to make the home sufficiently maintenance-free and functional so that you can be free to enjoy the country; to stretch space, to provide storage and accommodate weekend guests; to keep costs down but appearance up; and perhaps, above all, to work with local trades people whose metabolism is out of synchronization with yours.

The opportunities, however, can more than compensate for the aggravation. The decoration of a country home forces you to use your imagination, to experiment with new ideas, to improvise with what is available, and, best of all, to become involved in creative acts—finishing furniture, painting walls—which you may never have had the time, courage, or desire to undertake in your permanent residence. Couple this with the enjoyment of attending country auctions and the satisfaction of finding a conversation piece at a farmer's yard sale, and you can see how the decoration of a leisure home can be part of the fun and freedom of living in the country.

So if your country place is an unfurnished place, count your blessings.

DECORATING YOUR COUNTRY PLACE

CHAPTER ONE

FINDING AND FIXING UP
A COUNTRY HOME

The time to begin planning the decoration of your country home is when you begin looking for it. A mansion on a secluded island may be your dream house, but when you consider the cost of heating and furnishing all those rooms, you may discover why the owner is selling so cheap.

Location

The drive to get to the country can be great, unfortunately in more ways than one, so beware of impulse buying and do not become mesmerized by the first pleasing house you see. There are charming country houses everywhere; before choosing a location, consider the following questions:

Are you seeking a house for strictly seasonal use, such as winter skiing or summer sunning, or do you intend year-round visits? Obviously, an uninsulated house on the beach will not be suitable for the latter purpose.

Is the area adapted to your future needs? A house in the middle of nowhere may be perfect for a honeymoon, but when the children arrive, neighbors with children of similar age are a blessing.

Will long or short periods of time be spent there? Traveling back and forth to a distant spot can quickly nullify a weekend's rest. On the other hand, if you plan a week or month's stay at a time in your home, distance might be less important. So among the first things you should do is to

Ways to say welcome: *From top left clockwise*, a merry mailbox covered in self-adhesive plastic, a special sign, carved door with handsome hardware, a blackboard for messages, door decorations of gaily painted bells.

decide how far from your permanent residence you would like to be and what means of transportation is available to get there. Look at a map and mark a radius representing the distance or the time you are willing to travel; for example, the condition of roads, access by train, bus, plane, and projected plans for new roads and services are considerations that affect not only the ease with which a house is reached, but its potential for appreciation as an investment.

Other factors that should affect the choice of area include:

Proximity to recreational facilities, such as a beach, ski lift, golf course, tennis court, movie theaters (great for the children on rainy days).

Shopping and medical services: You can stock almost everything in a freezer, but if there are no stores nearby that carry milk and other perishables, you will be inconvenienced. Availability of medical services is also a necessity.

Climate: Although everyone hopes for skies free of clouds and insects, be realistic about the possibility of rain at the beach or mosquitoes at a lake.

Resale or rental potential: This is particularly important if you wish to be free to vacation elsewhere, such as Europe, on the rent from your country home. If your area is deteriorating or falling out of favor as a vacation resort, the chances of renting or selling your house will become less each year.

Having tentatively selected one or more locations, talk to people who live there, or better still, rent for a season before committing yourself to a purchase.

According to some real estate agencies, the best time to look for land or a house is off-season and not on weekends. For a summer house, the perfect time may be late fall or early winter (as long as houses are not covered with snow, which would impede full examination), thereby avoiding the spring rush.

First impressions are made in foyers: *At right*, in a writer's home, a bookrack guards the front door; in a designer's home (*facing page*), a large ottoman, carousel horse, and paintings purchased at an outdoor art show fill the entrance.

Buying a House

Evaluate the house in terms of the following, but then remember that nothing is perfect. Compromise. Evaluate what a change would cost. Sometimes a paint job can work miracles and is all that is necessary to modernize an old house; on the other hand, remodeling a bathroom can be expensive.

Here's a checklist of some things to look into; many relate to the building of a brand-new house as well:

1. *Location:* Within walking distance of town, beach, school? Secluded? Will transportation and security be a problem?

2. *The orientation of the house:*

—To the street, to other houses, to the road? Is there a

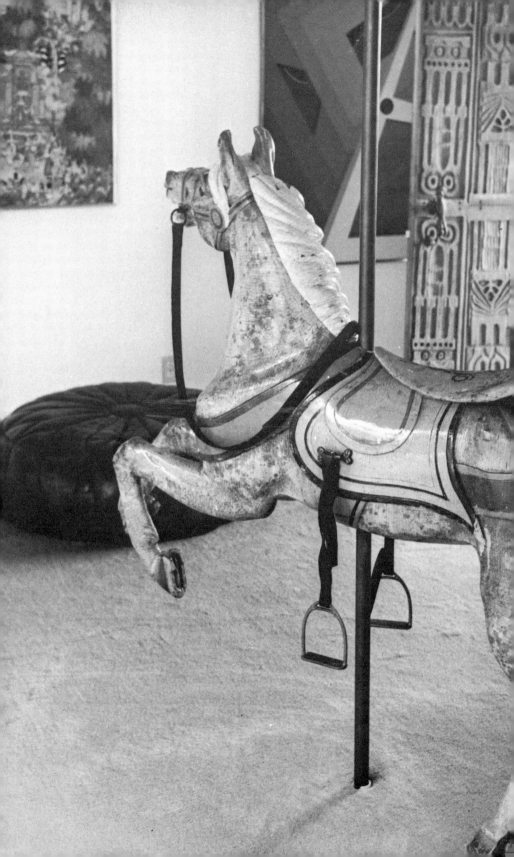

great deal of traffic, many neighbors? Who owns the road and who maintains it? At a ski house will there be a problem of access in heavy snow?

—To the prevailing breeze and sun?

3. *Age:* A new house will be in move-in condition, with new plumbing, heating, and electrical systems, shiny new appliances, and no modernizing or repairs to keep you busy on weekends. That's good because you will need the time to landscape and put down a patio floor—outdoor areas are usually neglected and undeveloped in new homes. When you go inside to rest, you can work on the windows and doors that are sticking because the house is settling or start to build extra shelves for the closets.

If you buy an old house, on the other hand, it may have these extra features probably at no additional cost: more space and character; beautiful, fully developed landscaping and outdoor seating areas; better construction materials, workmanship, and attention to detail (like an old piece of furniture); some furnishings, including built-ins in closets, and floor and wall coverings; but it may also have less desirable characteristics such as leaking pipes, extra halls and stairs to clean, and lights on pull chains. An old house usually requires some form of modernization—new appliances or bathrooms, modern plumbing, heating or electrical systems. Often the defects are hidden. You'll have a better chance with an old house if someone has recently lived in it, particularly if some improvements have already been made.

4. *What it comes with—furnishings:* What does it mean when the agent tells you the house is furnished or semifurnished? The furnishings you see in a "furnished" house may not all be included in the price; some may be "personal property," leaving you with only two beds, a table, and a shovel. Better ask for a detailed, itemized list or photograph the contents yourself. A well-furnished house in move-in condition may cost more, but it will be worth it because there will be no decorating problems. However, if

you do not like the furnishings, then you shouldn't pay a premium, for example, for pink shag wall-to-wall carpeting in every room, including the kitchen; then you must obviously add on the cost of new furnishings both in dollars and in time to the original cost of the house.

Furnishings may also include basic built-ins (beds, banquettes, bars, and bookcases), fitted closets, floor, wall and window coverings, fixtures, appliances, storm windows and screens, and gardening equipment.

If the house is in a resort development and has not been completed, you may have the option of choosing the color and style of some of these things, including kitchen and bathroom fixtures, appliances, cabinets, and tile.

5. *Utilities*:

—Heating: What kind of system (electric, gas, or oil) and what does it cost? A big barn of a house may be prohibitive to heat year-round; on the other hand, sometimes part of a large house can be closed off in cold weather. If there is no heating, and the house is exposed to the dampness of the beach or the coldness of the mountains or you want to extend the length of time it can be occupied, consider how much a heating system will cost and whether the house will have to be insulated.

—Electrical: What kind of electrical service? Sixty amperes is considered low for a full-time house but may be adequate for a country home; 100 to 200 amperes is preferable and necessary if you have heavy-duty appliances such as an electric range, clothes washer and dryer, dishwasher, and air conditioner. What is the location of switches, fixtures, and outlets outdoors as well as indoors? Are there old-fashioned pull cords? Not enough outlets? If there is no electricity, how far is it to the electrical lines?

—Plumbing: What kind of sewage-septic tank, cesspool, or city sewer? Water from a well, spring, stream, or city? Is there an irrigation system for watering the lawn?

6. *The placement of the rooms:* A country house filled with kids doesn't have to mean twenty-four-hour together-

ness and an end to sleeping late. The flow of traffic, how the space within a house is arranged, can make the difference. While there is a great deal to be said for the easy care of a compact efficient home, you have to be neat to live in one. So here are some more things to think about in the design of a house:

—Living and sleeping areas should be separated. Too much of an open plan can be noisy and lacking in privacy. Ideally, kids and guests should be away from the master bedroom area, or at least the placement of rooms should make this arrangement possible in the future. In a small up-and-down house it is better to put the children below the master bedroom—not overhead.

—The kitchen, in many ways the hub of activity of a home, should have a door that is near the garage or the driveway as well as within easy reach of dining areas, including outdoor eating places. A pass-through from kitchen to patio is a godsend.

—The main entrance is supposed to be near the driveway, but in my country house, which was prefabricated without thought to the site, it is on the other side, which means that all enter and leave through the back door, probably less embarrassing for a more meticulous housekeeper with a spotless kitchen.

—In a country home it is especially convenient to have bedroom, living room, or dining room doors that open out onto decks or patios.

—Access should be from one room to another without going through a third room. Bathrooms should be near bedrooms.

—The view and the amount of light and sun each room has should be considered as well.

7. *Rental potential:* By renting your home for part of the year and depreciating the purchase price plus the cost of furnishing, you can realize extra income and tax benefits that may, in part, cover carrying costs and have someone maintain the house when it would otherwise be empty. Fac-

INSPECTION CHECK LIST

TYPE:
SLAB ☐
RANCH ☐
COLONIAL ☐
SPLIT ☐
OTHER_____

Date_____

'or:_____   Location:_____

_____ _____
_____ _____
_____ _____

I. OUTSIDE

1. Ground Slope: Good____ Fair____ Poor____; Low Spots: Yes____; 2. No. Elec. Wires____ Over.____ Under.____
3. Termites: None apparent____ Evidences of____; _____
4. Exterior Walls: Brick____Wood Siding____ Wood/Asbestos Shingles____ Stucco____ Stone____ Other_____
   Condition: Good____ Fair____ Poor____; _____
5. Roof: Asphalt Shingles____ Slate____ Wood Shingles____ Rolled Roofing ____Tile____ Other_____
   Condition: Good____ Fair____ Poor____; _____
6. Gutters & Leaders: Copper____ Aluminum____ Galv.____ Wood____ None; ____ Drains/Dry Wells: Yes____ No____
   Conditions: Good____ Serviceable____ Poor____ Repair/Replacement. Yes____ No____
7. Putty: Serviceable____ Required____; Panes Cracked: Yes____ No____; ____ _____
8. Caulking: Serviceable____ Required____ At Chy.____; Diff. Mat.____; _____
9. Screens/Stormsash: Wood____ Alum.____ Steel____ None____ Not All____; Needed on Fixed Panes_____
   Condition: Good____ Serviceable____ Poor____; Repairs Indicated: Yes____ No____; _____
10. Exterior Paint: Good____ Fair____ Required____ on trim____ on exterior walls____; _____
11. Garage: Serviceable____ Poor____; Termite Evidence in Garage: Yes____No____; Not Visible____; _____
12. Trim Repairs/Replacement Indicated: Yes____No____ 13. Cracks in Found. Wall: Yes____No____Not Visible____

_____
_____
_____

II. CELLAR/UTILITY ROOM/CRAWL AREA

1. Walls: Concrete____ Block____ Stone____ Others____; Good____ Fair____Poor____; Cracks____
2. Evidence of Moisture-Seepage Penetration: Yes____No____; _____
3. Floor: Concrete____Other____; Good____ Fair____ Poor____; Cracks____Badly cracked____; _____
4. Termites: None apparent____ Evidences of____; _____
5. Columns: Steel____ Wood____ Other____ ____None____ Few Visible____ Not Visible____; ____
   Condition: Good____ Fair____ Poor____; _____
6. Girders: Steel____ Wood____ None____ (Not) (Part) Visible____; Cond: Good____ Fair____ Poor____
7. Floor Joists: Size & Spacing____; (Not) (Few) Visible____; Cond: Good____ Fair____ Poor____
8. Heating System: Oil____ Gas____ Other____; Hot Water____ Steam____Hot Air____; _____
   ____Condition: Operating____ Poor____; Needs Cleaning____
9. Hot Water System: Instant. w/Heating System____; Gas____Elec.____Oil____; _____
10. Plumbing: Copper____ Brass____ Galv. Iron____; Condition. Operating____Poor ____
    Plumbing repair Indicated: Yes____ No____; _____
11. Heating Unit Ventilation: Good____ Fair____ Poor____; 12. Door: Serviceable____ Poor____
13. Electric: Amperes____ Circuits____ Voltage: 220/110____ 110____; Main: Yes____ No____
    Wiring is: Adeq.____ Just Adeq.____ Inadeq.____ Rewire____; Circuits overfused: Yes____

_____
_____

III. ATTIC AREA

1. Roof Rafters: Size/Spacing____ Standard____ Below Standard____Recommend Collar Beams: Yes____
2. Insulation: Floor____ Walls____ Roof____ None____ Not Visible____; Good____ Adequate____ Just Adequate____
3. Floor Joists: Size & Spacing____; Flooring: Yes____ No____ Partial____
4. Ventilation: Adequate____ Inadeq.____ None____; 5. Roof Leaks: None apparent____Evidence of____
6. Hardware: Good____ Serviceable____ Poor____ None____; 7. Windows: No.____; _____

IV. REMARKS & SUGGESTIONS

_____
_____
_____
_____

ARTHUR TAUSCHER, PROF. ENGINEER 1958
HOME/BUILDING INSPECTION CONSULTANT

ROOM:_____

1. Ceiling: Plaster_____ Sheet Rock_____ Other_____ Papered_____ Painted_____
   Cracked: Yes_____ No____; Evidence of Leak:_____ Leak on Wall____ Ceiling____ Investigate__
2. Walls: Plaster_____ Sheet Rock_____ Tile_____ Other_____ Papered_____ Painted____
3. Windows: No._____; Weatherstripped: Yes_____ No_____; Cords Broken: Yes_____
4. Electric outlets: Number_____; _____
5. Floor: Wood____ Tile____ Concrete____; Condition: Good____ Fair____ Poor____; Slope: Yes_____
6. Trim: Wood_____ Tile_____ Steel_____ Condition: Good_____ Fair_____ Poor_____; ____
7. Hardware (locks, knobs, etc,): Condition: Good_____ Serviceable_____ Poor_____; ____
8. Heating Number___; Radiators____ Convectors____ Grills____ Baseboard____ Rad. H't'g____ Pipe Riser___
9. Doors: Exter.____ Weatherstripped: Yes____ No___ Cond: Good____ Fair____ Poor___; Need Adj./Repair: Yes__
   Interior_____ Cond: Good_____ Fair_____ Poor_____; Need Adj./Repair: Yes__
10. Plumbing fixtures: Yes_____ No_____; Good_____ Operating_____ Poor_____; Faucet Leak: Yes__
    Pressure: Normal_____ Below Normal_____; Grouting needed at tub/Shower Tile: Yes_____
11. Cabinets: Kitchen_____ Medicine_____ None_____
12. Stove_____ (Gas_____ Elec._____) Refrigerator_____ None_____; Good_____ Operating_____ Old____
13. Fireplace: Yes_____ No_____; Good_____ Serviceable_____ Poor_____; Damper needs repairs: Yes__

tors that affect rental potential include location and whether the house is heated. When furnishing a house that will be rented part of the time, the owner should set aside a place to store and lock up personal possessions and choose furniture that can be left behind without fear. However, according to real estate agents, charm has a price, and a well-furnished home can be rented at a premium.

8. *Ventilation and climate control:* The cliff dweller in his enthusiasm to capture as much sunlight and view as possible may choose an all-glass home which, because glass is a poor insulator, becomes a hothouse in summer and very expensive to heat in winter.

Obvious as it may seem, a leisure home should be well ventilated—designed so that the windows catch the prevailing breezes. A deep roof overhang above the windows should block out the hot summer sun but let in the warm winter sun.

9. *Maintenance:* Even the most modest house can eat up an extraordinary amount of money. Therefore, before buying, ask to see the bills for heating, gardening, house painting, and other services. A house with painted siding, especially one exposed to the elements atop a hill or on the ocean, is not going to be inexpensive to maintain. All this is in addition to mortgage payments, insurance, and taxes.

10. *Future remodeling:* Even if your remodeling plans are a long way off, you should consider them before you buy for these reasons: It will be necessary to see if local building codes permit major improvements, such as an addition or a swimming pool. Some areas have sticky laws about tennis court fences. Once you apply for a building permit, plan on a visit from the tax collector and an increase in the assessment of the house, which means extra taxes. Incidentally, you may not want to remodel, but even the most innocent change can necessitate it. The purchase of a dishwasher can lead to a new hot-water heater, then to a new electrical system, to a new kitchen, and, before you know it, to a new wing!

Evaluating It

The purchase of a country home should be made with at least as much care as a permanent home because it is occupied part time and often subject to water and moisture damage. The best person to hire to check the house out structurally is a professional engineer. Find one through the personal recommendation of friends, architects or builders or look in the Yellow Pages under Building Inspection Services. One such company with offices in major cities throughout the country is called The Home Consultants of (*city*). The chart on pages 21 and 22 and letter that follows illustrate the thoroughness of a professional investigation which, according to Arthur Tauscher, the head of the company that supplied this material, generally costs under $100 (the price is based on the location and cost of the house). In the absence of a professional engineer, a contractor, as well as an architect or an appraiser from the bank that may supply the mortgage, may evaluate the house.

DEAR SIR:

Attached hereto you will find the inspection check list report which we made for your client, Mr. Betts.

The heating unit is in operating order. It is recommended,

however, that the oil burner and heating unit be cleaned and serviced for proper operation when the house is taken over, and this cleaning and servicing should include the motor, blower, filter, humidifier, etc.

The water well and pump for the house were turned off, as was the pump and well system used for landscaping purposes, and the systems were drained. It was therefore impossible for me to check the serviceability and operation of the pumps and the hot-water system or to check on water pressures, piping leaks, and the operation of the various fixtures. It is recommended that any contract your client enters into contain a clause or clauses which will provide for the proper operation of these features and, further, if any deficiencies are revealed at that time, same are to be corrected without expense to your client.

It is important to remember that heating water electrically is expensive and the recovery rate is poor.

The electrical system, consisting of a three wire service, 220–110 voltage, 9 circuits and with 60 amperes available, is just adequate to serve the needs of this house. Many major electrical appliances are now in use in this house, but if any additional equipment is desired, it is suggested that a competent electrician be consulted so that no one circuit becomes overloaded or to determine if additional circuits and power are necessary.

The foregoing report is furnished at your request in strict confidence by us as your agent and employee for your exclusive use as an aid in determining the physical condition of the subject premises. This report is intended to cover only such portions of the premises and the equipment therein as may be examined visually; and we warn you that although such premises and/or equipment may be in good condition when examined, the condition may change thereafter. Furthermore, this report is not to be used as a basis for determining the value of such premises or whether same is or is not to be purchased. This report is not to be construed as a guaranty or warranty of the premises or equipment therein or of their fitness for use.

It would be wise to have each of the present circuits fully identified so that your client will know what electrical load is on each circuit. The important point to remember is not to overload any one circuit, and if your client has any doubts about this item, it is suggested that a competent electrician be consulted.

The foundation wall, columns, girders, and floor joists are in good to fair condition.

There has been some normal settlement of this house, which is to be expected.

The interior walls and ceiling of this house are lined with sheet rock. A number of nails employed to fasten this sheet rock have a tendency to pop out. This condition is inherent with sheet rock construction. When the interior is redecorated, the painter will recess these nails and plaster over them so they will no longer be visible. The several cracks that have appeared in the sheet rock can be taken care of when redecorating.

The exterior sidewalls of the house are in good to fair condition; however, painting of the exterior wood trim should be accomplished as soon as possible for both the sake of appearance and preservation of the wood itself.

It is recommended that calking compound be placed around all window and door frames where they make contact with the sidewalls of the house. The vertical edges of the chimney, where they join the sidewalls of the house should also be calked. This calking work prevents drafts and moisture penetration. The putty work around individual window panes is, generally speaking, serviceable. Some touch-up work on this item, however, is indicated. The foregoing, although minor and inexpensively accomplished, is important.

None of the windows is equipped with storm windows. Installation of these will cut down drafts and loss of heat, besides adding materially to the comfort of the house. Storm windows are important because not all the windows are weatherstripped, and many are loose in their frames.

The drainage around the house can be classified as good to fair, but no evidence of water seepage or moisture was noted on the basement walls at the time of inspection. It was noted that the basement walls were recently painted. This would tend to cover up any moisture seepage condition that may exist.

The installation of a dehumidifier unit in the basement area is recommended.

Based on our observations on those portions of the house that were accessible, no active termites or termite action was apparent at the time of inspection. No probings were made in or on this house, nor were furnishings moved since this would tend to cause damage to same. With the present owner's belongings blocking areas of the basement, a complete inspection could not be performed.

The raised front entrance platform is a possible area of easy termite entry into this house. Further, it was noted that the top course of foundation wall blockwork was not filled solid with cement, so termite entry is possible. Thus, periodic termite inspections (every one to two years) of this house are recommended. This is normally done at no charge to the homeowners by exterminating firms. This is important because termite entry can be anticipated, and these inspections will detect the condition before any major damage can occur.

As an alternative, an antitermite chemical treatment of this house should be considered. This will halt any termite action that may be going on which is not detectable at this time.

Although "no evidence" of termite or termite damage is reported, because of the insidious habits of termites, no responsibility for a termite condition that may exist or may be starting and was not visible is assumed.

Gutter-leader repairs are indicated.

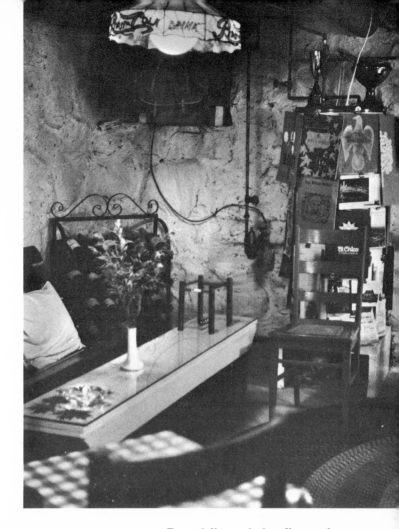

Remodeling a drab cellar need not be expensive or elaborate. With a bit of whimsy, the owner of this older house in the Adirondacks transformed a previously unusable space into a cheerful barroom. The hot-water tank is camouflaged with menus hung from magnetic hooks. Visitors autograph the heating ducts, and on the pipes a sign and decoy ducks are an effective warning. To lighten the room, stone walls were whitewashed, three Coca-Cola chandeliers were installed, tables were covered with red and white checked tablecloths, and the floor was covered with a braided rug. Furniture comes from an abandoned camp in the area.

Additional data concerning the house are noted on the individual inspection sheets, which will serve as a ready reference if your client purchases this house.

Unless otherwise noted on the inspection check sheets, none of the appliances was tested.

As a final word and speaking in general terms, the conditions found in this house can be described as being above average for a house of this type and age group.

Very truly yours,
Arthur Tauscher

If you must do it yourself, here are a few tips:

First, check the basement for evidence of flooding and for dampness and moisture. In a wooden house check for termites, carpenter ants, and dry rot by jabbing at wood structural members with an ice pick. An ice pick that goes in easily may mean trouble, but this can be corrected. By touching a simple magnet to the plumbing pipes you can tell whether they are made of iron or steel, which will react, or copper, which will not (copper pipes are superior and will last longer). Look for cracks in the foundation walls— look at the fuse box and outside the house at the electric meter to determine the kind of electrical service. Information about heating and plumbing can usually be obtained from the company that services the equipment in the house. Upstairs, close and open windows, flush toilets to test water pressure, look for cracks in the walls and signs of leaks such as brown spots on the ceiling. Determine the condition of the attic, if there is one, and whether or not it is too hot to be used for sleeping. Though you may not be able to test the appliances in the house, you can determine their age by the model number.

It is very hard to anticipate all the things that can go wrong in a house, and if you did, you would probably never buy one; however, it does help if you can arrange to rent with an option to buy before making a final commitment.

Similarly, live in a house if possible before remodeling or redecorating to determine your needs accurately.

Unless you pay all cash, you will have to arrange for a mortgage. Your real estate agent may be able to suggest a local bank, but in some cases you may prefer to deal with your own bank. Between the bank and your lawyer a title search will be made, assorted insurance issued, and a closing date arranged. By the time the house changes hands the old owner should have given you:

—Instructions on how things in the house work.

—A list of all service people.

—All sets of keys that he has.

—The location of underground utilities, such as the septic tank and well.

—Old plans and blueprints of the house if he has them (if he does not, the builder, local building department or architect may have a set).

You should also arrange to split the cost of services such as electricity that span both ownerships, so that the service is not discontinued. This is more than a matter of convenience. The former owner could have the electricity shut off on the day he sells—and by the time the new owner has had it reconnected, all the pipes could have frozen and burst, destroying walls and floors and creating chaos and extra costs for the now not-so-happy new homeowner.

RESORT CONDOMINIUMS

I would like to add a brief word about resort condominiums or developments of vacation homes and apartments. Maintenance and renting programs run by a hotel or central management and good recreation facilities make this kind of purchase very attractive. In addition, the vacation home can become income-producing as a rental property, and the owner can get substantial tax benefits by depreciating both the purchase price and the price of furniture and fixtures.

Different ways to decorate sta
cases: *From top left clockwise,* w
unframed family photos tacked
to wall; by painting treads a diff
ent color from the risers; with
lavabo planter and a ceiling-hu
painting on landing; with mu
colored braided linen runners; w
eclectic furnishings; with a bold
sign painted on.

To make it all work, the management must be efficient and honest. In a hotel/home complex, the hotel should be financially secure, so that one day you don't find that your investment in your home has been used to pay off the creditors of a now-bankrupt hotel.

Building and Remodeling

Building a country home can involve delays and disasters Mr. Blandings never even knew about, but these can be offset by the challenge of acquiring a home designed to your special needs and taste, with many of the decorative features built in. Some of the previous remarks apply to new houses and some of the following to old houses being remodeled.

Basically, houses either are built on a site, stick by stick, by a local builder/general contractor according to his plans, plans bought from a company, or architect's plans or are prebuilt in whole or in part and then shipped to and erected at the site according to the manufacturer's specifications. Factors affecting the kind of construction include speed, cost, design, and special problems of the area such as availability of manpower and materials, the condition of the site, zoning restrictions, and the weather (presence of snow, condition of roads, etc.).

Prebuilt houses come in degrees of finish, from loose lumber and materials factory cut in a kit, usually referred to as precut, to prefabricated from whole wall sections, to totally finished modular sections equipped with plumbing, wiring, even carpeting. One of their major advantages is that the buyer knows exactly what materials he is getting and how and where they will appear in the finished house, a particularly significant factor when building a house too far away to supervise. Unlike standard houses, which normally take at least three to six months to build and can take much longer in a resort area, a prefab is instant housing. Erected and ready for use, it is almost faster to get a house delivered today than a piece of furniture. This can mean an extra season in the sun to the country homeowner. Clearly, a mass-produced house is also going to be lower in cost, at least until it leaves the factory. In many cases, and you should check on this carefully, the trucking costs for prefabs can be prohibitive and sometimes they cannot be delivered at all owing to the inaccessibility of the site. Delivery costs and problems of a precut house are less of a factor. Endless numbers of extras can escalate the cost of prebuilt houses. On the other hand, a house that comes prebuilt and ready to assemble, or in varying degrees of togetherness, can be a challenging project for the do-it-yourselfer, aided perhaps by local electrician, plumber, and carpenter, and a good way to cut costs and to enjoy the country even when the house is just a shell.

Offsetting the advantages of prebuilt houses is the fact that they are designed miles away without any thought to a particular area or site. This means that the building materials may not be suited to the climate, and the orientation of the house and windows may not take into account the view, the location of the sun, and the direction of the prevailing breeze. A house made with nails that will rust at the seashore and picture windows that look out on the neighbors instead of the lake may not be worth the savings in time and cost. So, to be safe, show an architect, builder, or professional engineer the model or plans and specifications of the house. Ask for an evaluation and also a recommendation on the placement of the house on your property.

Building at its most efficient always seems to take more time and money than anticipated. No one should plan his vacation around a projected completion date unless he likes living with carpenters and plumbers and dodging the building inspector who is after him for moving into a house that does not have a certificate of occupancy.

HOW TO EXPEDITE BUILDING AND SAVE MONEY

Whether building or remodeling, to expedite the job, to avoid extra expense and to get it done properly:

—All written estimates should specify the complete cost of the job including the kind of materials, size, color, manufacturer number—and the cost of labor.

—Stock sizes and standard equipment are less expensive. These include windows, doors, glass, kitchen and bath equipment, and plumbing fixtures.

—Plumbing should be planned so there are as few pipes as possible by putting bathrooms and kitchens or other bathrooms back to back and fixtures on the same wall.

—All building should consider future outdoor as well as indoor furnishings, but it usually does not. This includes built-ins; floor and wall coverings; and the placement of heating and cooling units, electrical outlets, light fixtures, and telephone lines to conform and not interfere with the arrangement of furniture and appliances.

—New hallways and stairwells should be large enough to allow for the movement of furniture.

—Secondhand building materials are often both less costly and more distinguished than new ones. These include hardware, stained or plain glass windows, doors, plumbing and light fixtures, paneling, stair railings, and fireplace mantels. Sometimes costlier than new, but often worthwhile, are hand-hewn beams and barnboards. Add removal and delivery charges to the cost of secondhand material.

—Plan ahead and don't make changes.

—Try to be there yourself to supervise even if the architect or general contractor is on the job.

—New products are so plentiful that it is hard for the most informed professional to keep up with the market. If you want something special in color or design, you may have to do your own detective work. Become educated. Read building magazines; visit showrooms; write manufacturers for their catalogues. Always ask for specifications, sizes, and prices.

DOING IT YOURSELF

Speaking of doing it yourself, anyone who has built a house or remodeled must have thought at one point or another that he was doing it himself, or at least he might as well be, or if he was, at least it would get done. Well, if you actually *are* doing even a small part yourself, find the best lumberyard or building supply house in the area or in the nearest large city. It sells many supplies in addition to lumber, including nails, windows and doors (called millwork), insulation, wallboard, roofing material, cement, flue lines, cement block, and sometimes paint, ceramic tile, wall and floor coverings, and other decorative material. Order enough so you don't run out halfway through a weekend job. Ask for help during nonbusy hours and for a professional contractor's discount of 10 percent and follow instructions included with the materials. Establish whether cash-and-carry purchases (which may be cheaper but useless without a truck) are less expensive, when and where the yard or supply house delivers, and the cost. If you are building on a mountain peak, the truck may not be able to make the climb, which is exactly what happened to the most diehard do-it-yourself house builder I know. The lumberyard simply dumped all the materials at the bottom of the hill.

Does it pay to do it yourself? That depends on your goals and your ability. It took this man two years to build his house, including the time it took to get the building materials up the hill, but it cost only one-fifth of what it would have otherwise cost. Was it worth it? Not only saving money but doing it yourself is part of the fun and freedom of owning a country house. There are many jobs to keep one busy building or finishing a house, and the major ones, such as electrical wiring and plumbing should probably be left to the experts. It's not just a matter of the lights going on when the toilet is flushed—or by themselves; electrical wiring installed by an amateur can be a fire hazard. And a licensed contractor may not want to become involved with straightening out a do-it-yourself project gone sour because the fire underwriters will hold him responsible for the entire job. Savings in money may be minimal, if any. The nonprofessional pays retail for electrical supplies but the contractor pays wholesale and makes his profit by charging the customer for his labor through the difference.

Many people have tried to economize by becoming their own general contractor. To do this, you must be at the site constantly so not a minute is missed of the daily aggravation of coordinating and coercing the myriad of trades involved in building a house, and these subcontractors may charge you more into the bargain than a general contractor.

Help! Contractors, Architects, Interior Designers, and Workmen

HIRING A GENERAL CONTRACTOR (BUILDER)

Even if you are planning to do some of the work yourself, a general contractor can be hired to do part of the job, or you can hand the whole thing over to him. That does not mean your cares are over; as a matter of fact, they are probably just beginning. Special attention to the choice of contractor should be given particularly if you are too far from the site to supervise.

—First, reread how to expedite building and save money, p. 34 .

—Determine the contractor's method of charging— usually either a flat price or an hourly charge based on time plus materials, with a maximum price "it will not be more than $————." The only thing you may get from a contractor who quotes a very low price may be inferior products and workmanship.

—Specifications and plans can be bought from building companies or architects, or the contractor may supply you with them. Some contractors are also architects. If the contractor is involved in the design of the project, you should of course be on the same wavelength esthetically.

—Check out his reputation locally with former customers. (Did he show up on time? Did he finish when promised? Did he keep to the estimate? What was the quality of his work?) And check on his credit with the local bank and lumberyard.

—Try to pay in installments, withholding as much money as your conscience will allow until the job is finished, the last nail pounded in, and you are fully satisfied.

—If you are on the job *personally*, check with the workmen before they begin work each morning to find out *exactly* what materials they are using and what they are doing with them—not just "putting in a door," but exactly where and which one.

In case you think all this is splitting hairs, here's a true-to-life horror story guaranteed to make those hairs stand on end: This is about the routine remodeling of a carriage house. To begin with it took many persistent phone calls to get the job started. Then, after a brief appearance the contractor disappeared, and when he finally reappeared he doubled his time charges. From then on it was all downhill. The contractor didn't order enough floor tile (which delayed the entire remodeling for weeks) and installed new windows and doors that did not match the old ones in the house (at what seemed to be arbitrary heights that had no relation to other doors or windows in the room or to each other). In the kitchen he ordered and hung cabinets that were the wrong size, forgot to leave enough room for an eating bar or for appliances which now extend out further than the counter (which came in the wrong color) and installed new plumbing without bothering to see if there was plumbing nearby, and there was. There's more to the story, but I think the point is made.

ABOUT ARCHITECTS

Similar guidelines to those mentioned for hiring a contractor apply to the hiring of an architect, only more so. Check his reputation, his design ability, his compatibility with your own tastes, and his fees (flat fee plus expenses, a percentage of the total construction cost, an hourly basis against an upset or maximum price, or a fee based on time and materials).

Standard operating procedure should include the following:

—Initial interview: Discussion of client's needs (space, low maintenance), budget (plan on spending much more), likes and dislikes, including the kinds of building materials preferred.

—Preliminary plans: Presentation of rough plan with rooms and spaces blocked out, location of utilities, outlets (location and number) of house on site, and rough idea of cost.

—Detailed drawings and lists of specifications and materials submitted to general contractors for bids. If the building cost is too high, changes are made. The general contractor is then chosen, and he works under the supervision of the architect.

The advantages of working with a local architect when it comes to the daily supervision of a large job or the building of an entire house are evident. However, this is often not possible. If the architect is from your hometown, he may simply hand over completed plans and specifications to the general contractor and do little or no supervision of the job.

While an architect is usually hired to design the entire house, some are willing to act as consultants for a flat fee or hourly charge and to give advice on specific building, decorating, or remodeling problems. It is particularly helpful, and money well spent, for the country homeowner to be able to hire a local architect familiar with special problems of the area, such as the zoning laws and the climate, even if it's just to give advice about the installation of one thing, for example, a quarry tile floor.

INTERIOR DESIGNERS

The furnishings for a country home will often be selected by the owner, previous owner, or the architect, but an interior designer may also be hired to help. And while you might never consider using a designer at home, there are certain advantages to using one in the country. A local designer, particularly in a resort area near a large city—for example, Miami—will be familiar with local resources and be able to do much of the buying for you. In your absence the designer or the design staff of a department store can supervise delivery and installation of furnishings.

On the other hand, local talent may be scarce and you may prefer to work with a designer from your home city. Shopping may be more convenient and the selection of furnishings better. For problems of delivery and costs, see p. 127.

To find an interior designer get names from friends, professional organizations, and home magazines. Look at his work, the homes he's furnished, find out if he's available and how long the job will take. Establish your emotional and esthetic compatibility. Discuss budget. Since designers have radically different fees—based on a percentage of the cost of furnishings or on time charges—comparison shop, and don't forget to ask about charges for traveling to your country home, if this is necessary. Travel costs can be high especially if the home is far away and the designer must make one or more trips to measure, buy furniture, or supervise decoration. Even travel to a nearby area can take the designer away from his office for a day, and this translates into many extra dollars of expense.

As in the case of architects, a designer may be hired to do a lot or a little—for example, the selection of furnishings only or the selection and purchasing of all furnishings, supervision of delivery and installation and handling of complaints and problems along the way. The designer may do a complete home or just a room, work from scratch or with what you already own. A talented designer can, within a few hours of consultation, select wallpaper, fabric, and colors which will quickly and inexpensively transform old hand-me-downs or tell you now to rearrange and re-cover the contents of a home bought furnished and then leave you on your own to do buying and follow up.

A FINAL WORD ON WORKMEN

I would like to end this chapter with some answers I received from country homeowners when I asked the question "What difficulties have you had with workmen and how have you overcome them?"

Answer: "Great patience and a sense of humor are the only ways to deal with local talent. And an ability to explain to a husband who cannot understand a no-show. This never happens in his office!"

Answer: "After living in an area for a while, one learns who is reliable and who is not. Billing procedures are bizarre. One may not receive bills for years."

Answer: "Architects died, were drafted, or moved. The workmen were fine. The materials supply was slow, and we never did solve this problem."

Answer: "Make friends of workmen, but still prod them, hold money back, and call in the early morning or late the night before to find out if they're coming."

Answer: "Buy a lot of do-it-yourself books. Become reasonably competent in simple plumbing, electrical work, carpentry, painting, and landscaping skills." (See bibliography for recommended books.)

Answer: "I don't know what to do about it except cry a lot."

To these words of woe and wisdom I would like to add my own. It is possible to find great craftsmanship and loyalty among local tradespeople; on the other hand, poor workmanship and lack of responsibility are not uncommon. No matter whom you are hiring and what they are doing, whether it is fixing the toilet or raising the roof, try to pick the best around for the money. Ask friends, the previous owner, neighbors, local shop owners, and dealers for recommendations. As a last resort, look at advertisements in newspapers and listings in the Yellow Pages. Ask for references. Verify their ability and reliability. Commit to writing what they are to do, including the complete cost of labor and materials. In other words, if a painter is painting a house, establish whether the price includes paint and repairing plaster. Be sure to get a workman's address in case something runs afoul. Withhold all or as much money as you can until the job is completed. Don't take your eyes off him if he shows up!

To avoid the crunch, and whenever possible, try to schedule work off-season, when it is easier to find workmen and at better prices. At the height of the season in many vacation areas you will be lucky to get your hands on a breathing body, and you will happily pay any price. If the job is not a highly technical one, competent amateurs, students looking for extra cash, are a good source of labor and are usually plentiful in the summer and during vacations. Import your own if there is nobody in the area to do the job and you don't want to do it yourself. The extra cost of transporting and housing your hometown painter or tiler may not be as prohibitive as you think and may pay off in a better-quality job.

Extra Advice: If you plan to rent your house part of the time, try and find a tenant who will renovate or decorate in exchange for free or reduced rent.

A simple but elegant alternative to remodeling: Hide a bedroom bathtub behind a screen instead of removing it and building a new bathroom.

CHAPTER TWO

COUNTRY KITCHENS AND BATHROOMS

Whether your house is old or new, built or bought, you may have to sink money into your kitchen and bathrooms.

General Considerations

—Bathrooms and kitchens should have day and artificial light and good ventilation; if not a window, then at least an exhaust fan.

—Try to use standard-sized equipment and stock cabinets. For example, it may be cheaper and easier to buy a new sink and cabinet combination unit for bathroom or kitchen than to build custom-size cabinets around an existing sink.

—Secondhand equipment should be very inexpensive and in mint condition to make it a worthwhile purchase. The cost of removing and replacing fixtures and appliances can be high, sometimes more than the equipment itself.

—Keep plumbing costs down by installing new equipment where the old was.

—Try to relate the design of the kitchen or bathroom to the adjacent room or area. In an open plan, for example, the kitchen should be built or decorated as part of the dining room-living room with the same or similar floor and wall coverings. This can also be achieved simply by using coordinated colors or fabrics, for example, the same curtain in kitchen or bathroom as in adjacent rooms.

43

—Sometimes a minor reorganization like the relocation or redesign of a door can easily and inexpensively solve a space problem, such as not enough room in the kitchen for an eating surface. And if space is at a premium, items that are normally stored in a kitchen or bath may be kept outside in a nearby closet.

—Appliances bought and installed locally may be easier to have serviced or to exchange if defective.

—When ordering new fixtures, specify brand, style, and color and tell the plumber *exactly* where to install them. Allow for the time you will be without an appliance or fixture that is being replaced, such as a stove.

—Put color in easily replaceable areas, at the windows or on floors and walls. Colored fixtures are more expensive and involve a lifetime commitment—very few people can afford to buy new fixtures just because they get tired of the color. In addition, it is difficult to match the color of one fixture to another made by a different manufacturer.

Rejuvenating Without Remodeling

These easy and inexpensive ideas suggest alternatives to remodeling:

—Add a new floor covering.

—Paint, paper, or panel the walls.

—Change the window treatment: add new curtains, shutters or shades.

—Fabric or paper coordinate walls, windows, seat covers, or shower curtains.

—Repaint cabinets, or decorate them with wallpaper or self-adhesive plastic.

—Cover old wall tile and appliances with enamel paint (test first), epoxy paint, or self-adhesive plastic.

—Patch chipped fixtures with a compound, generally called a porcelain or appliance touch-up.

—In a bathroom paint the outer surface of sink and tub and toilet cover with high-gloss enamel paint or epoxy

Easy and inexpensive ideas for rejuvenating bathrooms: *Top left*, use accessories like picture frames, in unusual ways, as towel holders; *top right*, use matching accessories, toilet seat, wastebasket, shower curtain. A piece of chain holds towels; *bottom left*, matching wallpaper and shade, shower and window curtain; *bottom right*, color-coordinated towels, in a stripe that echoes wallpaper, and a painted tub.

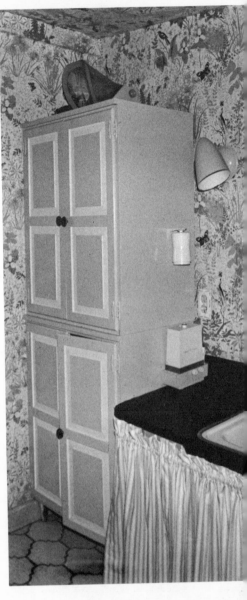

Bathroom storage: *Clockwise from top left.* Shelves over toilet hold linens— this mini area was created by curtaining off an alcove in the bedroom. • Two cabinets piggyback give double the storage in a single space. More storage is below curtained sink. • In place of medicine cabinet, toiletries are kept on exposed beams

paint; build cabinets or put a skirt around the sink bottom. Add a beautiful shower curtain.

—Change accessories, add new lighting fixtures or antique ones, some colorful pictures, a bunch of flowers, or a row of plants, an offbeat towel holder, some brand-new hardware.

—For extra storage and decorating appeal, include interesting furniture—an old chest of drawers, cabinet, or bookcase. Be sure pieces are easy to clean and, if necessary, cover with washable and heat-resistant tops of glass, marble, or self-adhesive plastic.

Planning and Equipping Your Kitchen

You may only have to replace an appliance, close off a kitchen area, add new cabinets. But what appears at first to be a minor face-lift can suddenly turn into major surgery for the kitchen! So be prepared.

Kitchen Equipment

1. *Cabinets and storage:* For food, cooking utensils, dishes, and flatware, cleaning tools should be kept as near to where they will be used as possible: in cabinets, on walls and floors, and—don't forget—in drawers. Extra storage may be found in or below the stove, below the sink, above upper cabinets, on pegboard or hooks on the wall, and on shelves placed between wall studs. Shelves for canned goods can be as shallow as six inches. Open shelves are popular with neat people but terrible dust collectors. If your house is far from stores, adequate provision should be made for additional storage, like an extra-large freezing area in refrigerator, a separate freezer, and room to store nonrefrigerated food, some of it in airtight containers to protect against the invasion of rodents and insects.

Cabinets or shelves can be wood—left natural, stained, or painted—or metal, usually steel with a baked enamel finish.

Adding character to a kitchen: *Above*, a wallpaper used throughout this house is just as appropriate in the dining corner of this country kitchen. White wicker furniture, exposed and stained posts and beams, and terra-cotta floor tiles are pretty and practical. *Opposite, top left*, more imagination than money: a wall divider made from paper cups glued top to top and bottom to bottom, a flower holder cut from a Clorox bottle, a bookend that is an old pulley, and a wall decoration that is a serving platter. *Top, right*, antique accessories, wicker stools, and wrought-iron cooking utensils add charm to a plain Jane kitchen. For extra eating and seating space, a sliver of a counter and two simple stools. *Below left*, everything in sight, including the window shade, is covered in self-adhesive plastic (and out of sight, on the floor-to-ceiling wall storage unit). Old furniture was used as kitchen tables; pegboard, narrow shelves on doors, and a butcher's rack for additional storage.

Offbeat appliances: *Top*, a Garland restaurant stove in a house that was a former East Hampton Coast Guard station. *Bottom*, a refrigerator that hangs on the wall.

2. *Appliances:* In addition to standard sizes and models, many new styles, shapes, and combination models are available. For example, a stove, sink, and refrigerator all in one unit, or a model that is part stove and part dishwasher; undersized stoves and oversized commercial ones; a refrigerator and dryer that hang on the wall like a kitchen cabinet. Before buying a kitchen appliance, find out not only what is new but also if it can be easily serviced in your area.

Small appliances include iron, electric frying pan, broiler, and toaster. Under certain circumstances you may be able to avoid the purchase of duplicates and use those you already own in your second home also—for example, when your city home is unoccupied for the summer and the country home is closed for the winter. Obviously, if it's a weekend house, this will not do. Just imagine packing the toaster every time you went back and forth!

—Sinks may have a single or double bowl and be made of stainless steel, enameled cast iron, or porcelain on steel (the cheapest but the one that chips most easily). The sink may have two faucets—one for hot and one for cold—or one faucet that controls both; it may also be equipped with a spray.

—Stoves consist of a range top and an oven below. Some stoves are also made with an oven above, but don't buy one of these if you like steamed clams because there is not enough room between the range top and oven bottom for the pot. In a new kitchen a separate range top is usually installed in one location and a wall oven in another.

Ceramic-type range tops are expensive but elegant to look at. They are supposed to be easy to clean. However, some people believe they are harder to maintain because, unlike standard range tops, they are white and smooth and thus show every bit of dirt. Most models require special cooking utensils.

—Refrigerators must be large enough with ample freezer storage and be self-defrosting. Consider the swing of a re-

Kitchen eating areas: *Above, left,* a multipurpose work and eating area with desk incorporated into a wall of storage units, classic Saarinen pedestal chairs and table, flowered fabric on vertical shades and chair cushions. The floor in this area and in the kitchen is wood. *Right,* Bentwood-style chairs circle a table made from a butcher-block top and a cast-iron base. Light fixture is an inverted basket. *Below right,* cushion-topped built-in banquettes line corner walls, give a lot of seating in a limited area.

Clockwise from top, left: a simple statement, three old ice-cream-parlor chairs, three hanging lights surround an eating bar that is also the divider between kitchen and living area • Wallpaper that looks like Delft tile and vinyl tiles that look like brick mix well with fine nineteenth-century furniture, a *vaisselier* (similar to a hutch) and a table that was once used for wine tasting • A bar carved from a tree • Pull up a stool to a butcher-block table for an instant eating area (wall decorations are painted wood cut out in the shape of fruits).

frigerator door and which will be most convenient, a door that opens to the left or to the right. An ice maker is a nice luxury.

—Washing machines and dryers can be top- or front-load-ing, separate units, or combination models practical in limited space. Portable washers (including dishwasher) are sometimes more trouble than help, since they usurp the sink faucet and must be moved about.

Extra advice: If the kitchen is not closed off from the living room, the endless noise emanating from these machines may be bothersome, so you might plan to put this equipment elsewhere.

3. *Counters:* Counter surfaces can be made from the fol-lowing materials:

—Plastic laminate (Formica) is easy to clean and doesn't stain. It is heat-resistant, but it can burn, and sharp knives can cut it. Very hot pots should not be put down directly on plastic laminate but on either a trivet or a section of ceramic which can be inset into a plastic counter top.

—Butcher block looks great and is an excellent cutting surface, but it can stain, and hot utensils leave heat rings. To keep the wood from drying out, wipe it with salad or vege-table oil.

—Stainless steel is completely heat- and stain-resistant, the most durable but it is noisy and expensive and scratches (a textured rather than a smooth stainless is best).

—Sheet vinyl and linoleum have poor resistance to heat and cutting, but resist most stains and are easy to clean.

—Ceramic tile and marble (when properly sealed) are. resistant to everything and easy to clean, but are also hard on dishes, noisy, slippery when wet, and expensive. Un-sealed marble will stain.

—Self-adhesive plastic is used principally to renew old counters at a minimum expense. You can do it yourself very easily. Counters can be covered in the same pattern as walls. It is easy to clean but not resistant to very hot things or cutting, so it should be treated with kindness.

4. *Floors and walls:* Should be washable and resistant to grease, dirt and moisture. On walls use a semigloss or high-gloss enamel paint, self-adhesive plastic, vinyl, or a washable wall paper. On floors use a resilient floor covering (see p. 169), ceramic tile (this can be hard on feet and dropped dishes), wood properly sealed or kitchen carpeting which feels good underfoot.

THE KITCHEN PLAN

In his desire to escape the cramped quarters of an apartment kitchen-in-a-closet, the owner of a second home may dream of rattling around in a vast expanse of kitchen. Hiking back and forth can be tiring, and since the whole point is to get a rest, the kitchen, especially a big one, should be carefully planned. Cabinets and appliances should be arranged whenever possible in a convenient order. It's easy to do this in a kitchen built from scratch; in an old kitchen, you have to plan around existing appliances, beams, radiators, windows and plumbing which cannot be moved or which you do not want to move because of the cost.

—The four basic layouts are U plan, L plan, double strip (row) plan, and strip plan (which could also be one free-standing row in a room, the room side an eating counter or serving bar). If possible, arrange appliances and cabinets so that the corner space is not wasted.

—Most base cabinets and appliances are 36 inches high and 25 inches deep.

—The stove should not be under a window (save this spot for the sink) and, if possible, not next to the sink or a door. There should be at least a little counter space on each side of the stove.

—It's preferable to put the refrigerator at one end of the counter and not in the center.

—The dishwasher should be near the sink and the cabinet that holds dishes.

Pass-throughs: Views
pass-through, the first
the dining-area side w
glasses are stored in a ca
above it, the second from
kitchen side where drink
prepared. A small refri
tor is in cabinet below.

Two roll-up matchstick
shades (one covers the en-
tranceway) conceal kitchen,
when desirable.

—Upper cabinets should be within an easy stretch but not too near the stove top.

—Allow enough clearance for opening dishwasher, refrigerator, cabinet and stove doors and for access to cabinets or other appliances.

The kitchen plan might also include room for a telephone, desk, and eating surface—anything from a large dining table or a counter to a narrow drop-down table that takes up practically no room and disappears when not in use. In a country home it's particularly nice to have easy access from the kitchen to outdoor dining areas through a pass-through or opening. For privacy, this opening can be closed off with shades or shutters.

Kitchen Contractors

Planning a successful kitchen is an art in itself. Many general contractors and architects acknowledge this fact and call in a kitchen subcontractor to help; unfortunately, not enough kitchen cabinet salesmen do. They pretend to know what they are doing. Since this is the area in the home where the most money is spent, it is wise to do your homework and bring to the remodeling—no matter how small— as much information as possible.

When I decided to remodel the kitchen in my country home, I called in what I thought to be a kitchen specialist from a store nearby—one that was part of a very large and well-known chain. I assumed that he would be the most experienced and most reasonable. This "specialist" must have been a lawn mower salesman, filling in. He was inexperienced and more interested in selling the maximum number of cabinets and appliances than in the utility of the kitchen. His plan would have placed a dishwasher in a ridiculous location. When opened, you couldn't pass by it, reach the sink to rinse off the dishes (which he said was "old-fashioned—nobody did that anymore"), or reach the cabinet above to put away the dishes. My suspicion that this

Two Fire Island kitchens: *Above*, area above and below work counter is open and free of cabinets. *Below*, separated by only a work/storage/serving island, this kitchen is an integral part of the living room.

was not a company to do business with was confirmed when he asked for full payment in advance. Usually, a one-third deposit is all that is required.

A kitchen planner can be your builder or architect, a representative from a department store, an independent specialist either in town or country, or the local plumber. These persons may do one or all of the following: design the kitchen, coordinate the ordering and delivery of cabinets (which may or may not be made to order), appliances, or counters, and hire and supervise the labor force that does the installation. There may be a separate fee for the design, or it may be included free as part of the job. Ideally this specialist should come to your home and take all measurements himself, but if you are far away from help, you may have to bring your plans to him. Since there is a very wide choice of appliances and cabinets at many different prices, just keep prodding if you aren't satisfied with his initial suggestions.

You will normally have a contract, and it should clearly designate all work to be done, including electrical, plumbing, plastering, and the removal of old equipment. It will, of course, specify the new equipment ordered and should give style, price, finish, and any other relevant information. The contract may indicate what will *not* be done, such as lighting.

And a crafty salesman will not bother to point out that you will need floor and wall coverings to fill in empty spaces that will be left after old is replaced with new.

Finally, read the terms of payment carefully before you sign.

Planning and Equipping Your Bathroom

As in the case of kitchens, the design or redesign of the bathroom may be a matter of degree. If a complete overhaul is required, the same firm that installs kitchen equipment can help you plan the bathroom.

In a home at a beach or lake area or one that has a swim-

Proof that there's plenty of room for imagination in planning a new kitchen: Parts of this one come from a butcher shop—the metal walls, the sink that was converted from a sausage table, and all the butcher blocks. The old doors in the rear were salvaged from a 1937 hurricane in the Hamptons. A coatrack of steer horns holds towels.

Below, another view of the kitchen reveals a brick island with Franklin stove and range top set into it. Copper pots hanging from old beams complete the effect.

ming pool, it is wise to plan for an outdoor bathing facility, just a shower or complete bathhouse. In some cases, this may be achieved simply by adding an outside door to a new or existing ground-floor bathroom. It's another door to lock but a good way to keep the house clean.

BATHROOM EQUIPMENT

While the following information is for standard equipment, I would like to point out that there are many design possibilities and unusual treatments available—especially for a brand-new bathroom—everything from an inexpensive all-in-one prefabricated plastic bathroom to elaborately tiled, custom-designed sunken tubs in the middle of the floor.

1. *Fixtures:* Bathtubs and showers—the standard-size bathtub is 5 feet x 30 inches x 16 inches or 14 inches deep. If the opportunity and the spirit are present, lie down in the tub and try it out for size before buying. An enamel on cast-iron tub is best, but porcelain on steel will do. Some prefabricated bathtub-shower combinations are fiber glass. Bathtubs can be glassed in or covered with a shower curtain. A stall shower prefabricated of fiber glass or metal can take up very little room.

—Sinks are available in many sizes and shapes, without legs (these hang on the wall and are easy to clean beneath) or with legs that stand on the floor or with a pedestal base. Some fit into corners. In addition to enamel on cast iron and porcelain on steel, sinks can be made of more costly materials such as stainless steel and vitreous china. There should be plenty of room under the spout for hands, in the bowl for washing clothes, and on the ledge surrounding the bowl for toiletries. If money and space allow, a double sink is a great convenience at bathroom rush hour.

—Toilets, like sinks, can stand on the floor or hang on the wall, and there are some models that fit into corners.

2. *Storage:* Plan for storage of linens, medicine, cos-

A simply super supergraphic in a spectacular poolhouse bath/dressing room incorporates pipes, sink and shelf unit, even bathing caps into the design. The wood floor is painted white.

A rustic outdoor shower with modest origins —some logs and a matchstick shade—help keep sand and dirt out of the house.

metics, cleaning supplies, magazines, books, and dirty and clean clothing. Shelves or cabinets can be put above the sink, toilet, or tub. Built-in cabinets below a sink not only look neat but are a good place to find extra storage. Shelves and cabinets can be recessed into the wall between studs. In addition to the usual towel bars and hooks, a bathroom that services swimmers will need hanging places for bathing suits and extra towels.

3. *Counters:* Counters make an old bathroom look new and any bathroom look neat and efficient. Any of the materials mentioned for kitchen counters (p. 54) will do even better here since water damage is the only enemy. If you are worried about a slippery surface, avoid marble (which you should also avoid if you are worried about money) and shiny glazed tiles (choose them with a mat finish instead), even more important when these materials are used as floor coverings.

4. *Walls and floors:* Bathroom walls and floors should be waterproof enough so that if they do 'get soaked they will not be ruined. Where you need more protection from water,

The design of the bathroom is as important today as the furnishing of more public rooms. With private walled-in sun deck, the one shown above is spacious enough to contain a freestanding bathtub in the center and a large makeup area. *Above, right,* large bird tiles distinguish a tile wall. *Below, right,* floral tiles set off a sunken tub.

A delightful duo, two sinks and two mirrors for double the convenience, especially at the morning rush hour. Tied-back curtains frame entrance and bathtub; the peacock chair is an elegant accent.

around the sink, tub, and shower, ceramic tile walls are the traditional covering. With the possible exception of the shower area you could probably safely use any of the following on the walls: plastic tiles (these come in self-adhesive, do-it-yourself form), vinyl, washable wallpaper, plastic laminate or water-resistant paneling, or paint (semi- or high-gloss enamel).

Traditional floor coverings include tiles, terrazzo, and marble, but other materials such as slate, wood, quarry tiles, and brick can be installed if they are properly sealed. Resilient floor materials such as vinyl and vinyl asbestos can cover an existing floor, but sheet form is preferable as water will seep into the cracks between tiles.

Do-it-yourself cotton carpeting made for this purpose can also effectively cover an old floor, quickly and inexpensively. It is best used where there is not too much traffic, for example, in a guest bathroom. It's not quite as easy as it looks to cut the rug to fit snugly around bathroom fixtures, so the unhandyman may want to settle for a gay oversized bathmat instead.

THE BATHROOM PLAN

The smallest area which all the above equipment can be squeezed into is 5 x 7 feet.

—Try not to scatter the plumbing; put it on one or two adjacent walls;

—Put the sink near a source of direct light and preferably next to a window.

—A large mirror over the sink not only is practical, but will also enlarge the room visually.

—The bathtub should not be under a window; it's drafty. In addition, you'll have to get into the bathtub to close and open the window.

—If the bathroom is big enough, include some form of divider, either a decorative screen or a divider of shelves or a closet, between the toilet and the rest of the bathroom.

—If the bathroom is too small for a regular door that opens into the room, pocket or folding doors can be substituted.

Extra space for sleeping was created under the eaves on a balcony overlooking the living room of this Westhampton home. To avoid claustrophobia, the area is only partially enclosed with shutters (it cannot be seen from below). A large standing mirror adds to the illusion of spaciousness, as does the scale of the furniture, a metal bed with delicate lines and a tiny table.

CHAPTER THREE

SECRETS OF SPACE

In vacation homes, where space is scarce, but guests and bicycles are not, you will want to make the most of what you have. This chapter is about measuring, conserving, and stretching it.

Taking Measurements

There is very little margin for error when you are buying furniture in one place for a house that may be very far away; if the new ping-pong table for the basement playroom won't fit down the basement steps, you are stuck. Therefore, measure your space and the furnishings you hope to use in it carefully.

To measure furniture, a flexible metal tape is best. A cloth tape can be used but is not as accurate because cloth stretches, while a wood rule is too stiff for measuring upholstered pieces. Measure and note the overall height, the width from side to side and the depth first. Then take other measurements since it is difficult to anticipate all the problems that may arise in the future. For example, to tell whether a dining chair will be too low or too wide for your dining table, you must measure the height of the chair seat and the width of the legs of the table. Although there are fewer limitations on space outdoors, you should still measure carefully to make certain furniture can be arranged conveniently.

It's just as important to measure hand-me-down furniture

as new furniture. While you may not be spending money for the actual piece, you will be paying something, and in some cases quite a lot, to ship it to your country place. If it doesn't fit or looks oversized, you will probably also have to pay someone to cart it away.

Once you have managed to get it through the door, furniture should fit in the room so that people do not have to climb over chairs or move the bed to open windows or to gain access to dresser drawers. Furthermore, furniture should be arranged in a rational way so that people sitting on one side of the living room do not have to shout to people on the other side or use binoculars to watch television. It can be placed in a tight central grouping or more loosely around the edges of a room.

Above all, furniture arrangements should always be flexible and comfortable. Furniture is designed to conform to the measurements of the human body. The height of most desks or tables is 30 inches with about 25 inches allowed for leg clearance; a practical height for a coffee table is about 18 to 20 inches. The average seat of a chair is about 18 inches off the ground; the depth can vary from around 18 inches for an occasional or dining chair to 30 to 40 inches for a lounge chair or sofa (which could also be lower).

Typical sizes of basic indoor and outdoor furniture are as follows. The figures represent how much floor space each will take up in inches, not overall measurements:

 Beds (single): 30″, 33″, 36″, 39″ x 75″
  Full-size: 54″ x 75″
  Queen-size: 60″ x 80″
  King-size: 78″ x 80″
 Couch: 72″ to 84″ x 30″ to 40″
 Love seat: 54″ x 30″
 Chair for eating or sitting: 14″ to 24″ square
 Tables (based on a chair 16″ wide):
  Round: 48″ (for 6 to 8 people)
   36″ (for 4 to 6 people)
   24″ (for 2 people)

Calculate other sizes by multiplying the number to be seated by 6 or 7.

Rectangle: 72" x 36" (for 6 to 8 people)
72" x 36" (for 6 to 8 people)
24" x 24" (for 2 people)

Calculate other sizes by allowing 24" around the table per person.

Chaise longue or armchair and ottoman: 72" x 24"
Arm/lounge chair: 30" x 30"
End tables: 24" x 24", 18" x 30", 18" x 18"
Coffee table: 20" x 48"
Dresser: 18" x 72"
Small chest: 18" x 36"
Buffet: 18" x 48", 60"
Ping-Pong table: 108" x 60"—allow 7 feet of runback for each end and 5 feet at sides.
Billiard table: 4' to 5' x 7' to 10'—allow 5 feet for playing around table.
Card table: 30" x 30"

Floor Plans

Instead of bringing the furniture measurements to the house, you can bring the house to the furniture by making a floor plan. If you do not already have architects' plans or some other form of floor plan of your house, make your own this way:

Use plain paper or, preferably, graph paper, a pencil, and a metal tape or wood rule (use your feet only as a last resort!). Go around the room measuring near the floor from corner to corner and then in between, indicating windows, beams, radiators, and any permanent fixtures that will interfere with or affect furniture placement. Indicate the direction of a door swing. Also measure the wall areas, noting anything of importance that would not show on the floor plan, such as a protruding air conditioner or the height of a large window or the dimensions of a radiator. Measure doors, halls, and stairways that furniture must be moved through. Note this is in feet, not inches.

If you want a good preview of the room, you can cut out shapes representing your furniture to scale from graph paper and arrange them on your floor plan.

Your floor plan will tell you not only how much space you have and what will fit within it but also the size of areas you may be planning to cover with wallpaper, paint, or a floor covering. The floor and ceiling areas (number of square feet) are the width multiplied by the length of the room. One wall area would be either the length multiplied by the height or the width multiplied by the height. For information on quantities, see p.219, "Do It Yourself."

Extra Room and Guests

MULTIPURPOSE ROOMS AND FURNITURE

To achieve a more functional home and to reduce wasted space, use rooms and furniture for more than one purpose. A bedroom can double as an adult living room and a kitchen as a playroom. A friend of mine has a house with a carport that converts, with the addition of screens, to a porch in the summer.

Furniture that folds completely away when not in use or has parts that pull out or fold down is a great space saver, as is furniture that serves multiple functions, such as a desk by day that becomes a dining table at night.

ROOM FOR GUESTS

Even in the smallest country homes there is more room than meets the eye to accommodate all those visiting relatives (if you'd rather not know, skip this section). Beds, carefully disguised or hidden, can go just about any place, in alcoves and wide hallways, in the dining room or living

Sleeping bags laid on a gym mat are great fun for young overnight guests and practical as well—they're inexpensive, roll up, and store on closet shelf and match the bedspread/sheets of the bunks. To keep the occupant of the upper bed from rolling off, heavy cord was laced through large giant screw eyes in the side of the bed and in the ceiling.

Room for guests: Bunk beds, basically slabs of wood (possibly a flush door) topped with mattresses can be arranged in several ways to make the most of vertical space. *Above*, four beds along a windowed wall. *Below*, in a corner with a chest of drawers as the support for the upper bed. *Opposite, top left*, on different levels for sleeping for six (two additional beds that are not shown are to the right) in a small one room cabin.

Extra bedrooms and beds can be hidden or disguised: *Top right*, stored on the ceiling, this bed, which works on a pulley system can be lowered at bedtime. *Below left*, a king size mattress looks smaller when placed in a corner of a room and piled with pillows. The owners' collection of antique toys is displayed on a glass coffee table. *Below right*, a bed that pulls out like a drawer from under a platform. Sliding Soji panels to left close off area for sleeping.

room, and on lofts. In warm weather, guests can sleep on porches and decks. Or put the kids outside in a pup tent and your guests in their beds (this works only with kids who don't get middle-of-the-night spooks).

Two relevant bits of information: (1) the minimum sleeping surface for an adult—unless he's very skinny and you don't want him to come back—is 30 x 72 inches; (2) allow enough room in the area for a fold-away bed to open up.

Different kinds of extra beds:
—Murphy beds drop down from a wall cabinet or panel.
—Convertible sofas open up to become beds.
—Daybeds are really like a bed dressed up as a couch. They are usually twin size, but if a room is large enough, a queen or king size can be used also. Covered with a handsome throw, a plain-jane bed can become a roomy lounging area and a good substitute for a couch. Placed in the corner of a room, even a supersized bed will not look as large; a corner bed should, however, have wheels or casters so it can be moved to be made up.
—Trundle beds have an extra one or two beds tucked beneath them.
—Bunks have an extra bed above them—they can have a trundle, as well. It is very hard to make the top bed.
—Built-in banquettes and mattresses or *one* large cushion (not several small ones)—wide and long enough for sleeping. This might double as your living or dining room seating made up at night for sleeping.
—Folding or collapsible beds include standard cots (I store two in my cellar for guests, move them upstairs when needed), metal army or canvas cots, sleeping bags, and air mattresses.

Expanding Space

To gain a feeling of space:
—Reduce the amount of furniture you have or think you

Space is stretched when a room is multipurpose like this combination bedroom/studio which functions twenty-four hours a day. Set apart from the rest of the house with an inspiring view and plenty of light, this room is perfect for both working and relaxing. A cork-covered work-and-storage area is on one side of a room divider that also contains a closet and shields the bathroom from view.

need. Some furniture can be stored when not in use. For example, here's how to make a dining room disappear: The table is a thin, narrow console pushed up against the wall and has an expansion top that opens at mealtime; a card table stores in the closet until dinner; a ping-pong table or work table is multipurpose; a narrow table with flip-top leaves opens and expands when necessary. Seats can be stools, folding chairs, benches, pillows, stacking chairs, or chairs from around the house. A serving bar can be a radiator top with a pretty cloth on top to hide its true identity or the top of a bookcase.

—Use vertical space. If the ceilings are high enough, create double-decker living, for example, a sleeping loft over the living room.

Expanding space: *Clockwise, from top left*, two small couches and extra ottomans that store under the coffee table provide ample seating for a small area • A cabinet built into the corner of a dining room holds a vast amount of tableware • A handy shelf and drawer was built in the normally wasted space between the end of the bed and the wall • A bed with drawers in the bottom holds clothing, toys, or linens, eliminates the need for a dresser. (Note the sticker decoration and posters tacked directly onto different colored walls.) • Between two closets, just enough space to fit a desk/dressing table • A storage and sleeping area in a boat is an excellent example of the ultimate use of space.

—Use built-ins that not only make a house look trim but reduce the need for free-standing furniture. Chests can be eliminated from bedrooms by being built into closets, or inexpensive unpainted chests or secondhand chests can be placed in closets. Our house came with some very ugly but spacious chests of drawers which are now built-in and hidden away in a closet.

—Bring the outdoors in with plenty of plants, bare windows and doors, by decorating with nature's colors, and by extending the same or similar wall and floor coverings from inside to outside.

—Keep the house color and pattern related by using the same or similar colors on walls and floors, ceilings and furniture. A harmonious or a monotone color scheme will heighten the feeling of spaciousness, as will soft diffused lighting.

—Use furniture light in feeling with simple lines or see-through furniture of clear plastic that is almost not there. The larger pieces in a room should be in inconspicuous places, perhaps in a corner.

—Mirrors add a great dimension of space if you don't mind spending your vacation keeping them unfogged and clean. Make sure, however, that what they reflect is worth seeing twice.

Hidden Storage

Even when a country house seems to have a great deal of storage, the amount can be misleading. A cavernous attic does not lend itself to the storage of gardening and sports equipment that is in frequent use, and in a country house in which there are growing children, your menagerie of bicycles and beach toys may soon exceed the accessible space.

Finding enough storage can be a matter of organization:

—First, throw out those extra eyesores that came with the house or all that junk that has just accumulated. Have a yard sale. Run an ad in the local paper and hang signs

Hidden storage: In a tiny niche, floor-to-ceiling shelves for bathroom
supplies are covered with a shade homemade from leftover wallpaper.

A brilliant solution to the problem of where to store fishing rods and reels—up high, over the door and down the hall. *Below*, storage shelves and cabinet for television built into wall.

around town, for example, in the grocery store. If you don't have enough merchandise, invite friends to clean out their clutter and join your sale. Freshen and price-tag everything; hold it for a day, at most two, and keep a record if more than one person's possessions are for sale; pray for a sunny day and a customer for that hand-me-down breakfront that wouldn't fit through the front door.

—Try to find extra storage areas—under the stairs, high in a hallway, between windows, under beds and couches.

—Separate the items to which you require frequent access from those to which you do not. Put out-of-season gear and clothing in boxes in the inaccessible attic or basement.

—Plan storage so that it will be close to the area it is used in. Garden and sports equipment should be near the outdoor play area—in a shed or in the garage. Skis on a rack; a bag for balls and mitts; outdoor clothing near the back door. Linens stored near or in bathrooms. If you disperse linens and supplies, the linen closet can be eliminated.

—Create extra storage spaces on walls and on the backs and fronts of doors by hanging things on hooks and on pegboard. For extra floor space, chests of drawers, shelves, and desks can also be hung on walls.

—Use furniture with maximum storage space inside it. That means no open bottom tables with skinny legs but chunky chests with drawers down to the floor. Beds with drawers in their bottoms hold a great deal and so do window seats with hinged tops and storage inside, as well as hampers and trunks that can do double duty as tables.

—Build a shallow storage wall the entire length of the room to hold a summer's worth of entertainment—hi-fi, books, bar, records—table linens and accessories.

—Plan and organize closets. The average closet is 2 feet deep and from 3 to 6 feet wide. About 7 feet is the highest an adult can reach, so anything higher would be in an area for dead storage. Types of closet doors that take up less space into a room than a standard swing door include: pocket in which the door slides into the wall, sliding, and

Closets: *Top left*, instead of a door, a curtain of beads. *Top right*, in a bedroom an island of closets is also headboard to the bed on the other side. *Below left*, closets with cabinets above them provide floor-to-ceiling storage. Doors are painted different colors. *Opposite*, a perfectly planned closet with hanging bars at two levels, and an old chest (instead of built-in doors), plenty of shelf space, and folding doors that allow maximum visibility and accessibility.

More storage: *Top, from left*, to protect an outdoor telephone at pool or dock from the elements, a country place of its own, perhaps, one that locks; • a large basket for storing sporting equipment; • under a low shelf/night table, large plastic bins (or cardboard cartons, wood crates) • a laundry and sewing center made by enclosing an unused alcove in a hall doesn't waste an inch of space. Narrow shelves on a mirrored wall hold liquor bottles, as well as cleaning supplies. Baskets for additional storage hang from the ceiling. *Below*, a ceramic grocery cabinet recessed into the wall above and cabinets below an eating bar.

folding doors or curtains, and these usually allow for a full view of the contents of the closet. But shelves, hooks, racks, can be hung only on a swinging door. Closets can be fitted with shelves and, as mentioned before, chests. All manner of things can be stored, from fishing rods to golf clubs to ping-pong table. Measure what is to be stored, and design the closet around this.

—If you don't have enough closets, you can buy metal or cardboard ones and, sometimes for the same price, antique armoires. Old clothespoles or wall racks are fine for temporary storage in an entrance hall or for guests.

—Extra closets can be used for a bar, an office, a music center, or a darkroom.

—If moisture is a problem, the closet door bottom can be louvered to let in air, an air duct installed in the closet ceiling or a dehumidifying rod hung in the closet. To allow for adequate air circulation around them, clothes should be hung loosely.

CHAPTER FOUR

FURNISHING

Your exhilaration at becoming a country homeowner is likely to disappear at the sight of those spacious but barren rooms that must be furnished by vacation time, without a furniture store nearby.

While some furnishings may be ordered from town, even if far away, there are many items to be found locally no matter where your home is located. Indeed, a large part of the fun of owning a country place, even one that comes furnished, is to scout antique shops, flea markets, auctions, and garage sales for the pieces that will give your home its unique character.

Make the most of the resources available. Staples like beds might be ordered from the nearest large city. A secondhand couch could be bought and re-covered locally; fabric for it purchased at home. You may even find a beautiful antique throw for the old chair you found in your mother's basement. Ask around for names of shops and tradespeople, and consult local advertisements and classified listings to see what and who are available.

While furniture gathered from assorted sources can make a house look like the Salvation Army showroom, it doesn't have to. There are certain commonsense rules to make a mixture work. The furniture should fit the house—not a lot of heavy upholstered pieces at a beach house or casual summer furniture at a ski lodge. It should be generally consistent in scale and degree of formality—not delicate satinwood with earthy pine or mostly heavy wood with a few

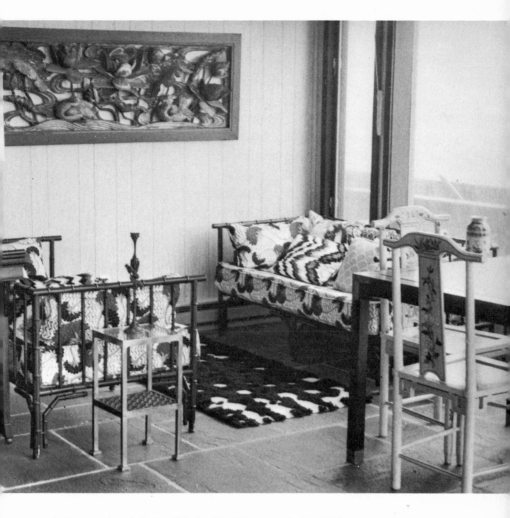

A Quogue beach house filled with Chinese-style furnishings: two metal "bamboo" settees, a card table and chairs, an altar table, and, on the wall, an antique Chinese wood carving.

Opposite page, top, modern furnishings are arranged on the diagonal in this Westchester pool house. A change in floor and ceiling height, as well as in floor material—from brick to wood—separates dining from living area (for photograph of pool house dressing room see p. 62). *Bottom,* with the exception of the deck chairs that came from the *Queen Mary,* giant pillows are the only seating in this living room. A collection of coral and a batik wall hanging decorate the fireplace.

spindly metal pieces thrown in. Textures, on the other hand, should vary, some hard ones like metal, marble, glass, and tile mixed with some soft ones like carpet, wood, and fabric. Old can mix with new very effectively. To make instant togetherness if the differences are too great, cover all furniture with the same fabric or paint.

Be prepared to put together unassembled furniture or furnishings that need installation, like bookshelves; otherwise, line up the local handyman or buy assembled or free-standing furniture like bookcases instead.

Time in a country place is precious, so whether it is something new or old, try to buy only what is ready to be carted home that day—by you or moving van. You will see exactly what you are getting and get it right away. No delays and no mistakes. If order you must, then plan to be patient.

Buying New Furniture

It may be easy enough to buy ready-made curtains and bedspreads, area rugs and pillows, but immediately available furniture you do not have to order is much harder to find. Many furniture and department stores and designer showrooms show samples only, and the customer orders from these. Naturally, if your house is only a hole in the ground today (which is when you should start to think about and order furniture anyway) or will not be occupied for many months, you can afford to wait.

Ironically, furnishings that are available immediately are usually less expensive. For example, fabric not normally available to the public except through a decorator or upholstery workroom can be bought at a mill end or remnant discount store, and the same department store that orders furnishings which take weeks or months to arrive may have a section of their furniture floor devoted to sale merchandise. If you are willing to buy remnants, "as is" merchandise, floor samples, or discontinued styles, you can begin to enjoy them immediately and at discount prices. This is an

Comfortable contemporary furniture surrounds fireplace. In the fireplace, a pair of four-foot-high Georgian cast-iron andirons, brought from Europe to this house in Long Island.

More formal rooms: This one is furnished with family heirlooms and, on a prayer stool, needlepoint by the man of the house.

Furnishings with a country French feeling around an ornate stove, the focal point of the room.

Outdoor furniture, indoors, perfect for a Palm Beach home. Circular carpet and seating piece in the living-room area are echoed by two round tables in the dining area. The walls were painted in stripes and in a trellisage pattern. *Below*, outdoor wicker gaily cushioned is at home inside this cabin in the Adirondacks.

Built-in furnishings: In a Bridgehampton home, wall-to-wall banquette for both sitting and sleeping and plants more plentiful than furniture.

In a Fire Island home, a tatami-covered seating platform topped with mattress, bolsters, and pillows, built in under a sloping wall.

In a peaceful beach house of Oriental design, notice the low dining table and chairs, the pile of floor pillows for extra seating, the giant paper globe, and, in the conversation pit, the cocktail tables that separate (for another view of the area to the rear, see the photograph on page 75).

Rustic pine furniture, an Oriental rug, and a big bin of wood are fitting furnishings for a Lake Placid "camp."

ideal source of furnishings for the country home since in a house that is not in full-time use, all the furnishings need not be perfect.

A country place should be a creative place, and there is nothing like need to shatter old decorating taboos and to stimulate imagination. If you are willing to be flexible, settling for a color or piece of furniture that isn't exactly what you had in mind, you will best be able to take advantage of what is available. For example:

If you cannot find a couch, consider as a substitute a hammock, a park bench, or even an array of pillows on the floor.

If you want a pattern on the wall but there are no wallpaper stores nearby, dream up your own design and paint it on.

If you need curtains and only shower curtains are available at the general store—well, why not? In this way, your home not only will be furnished faster for less money but will have a more distinctive character.

WHERE TO FIND FURNITURE

—Department and furniture stores: As mentioned above, look at the sale section if you want fast service.

—Carpet, wallpaper, and fabric stores: There are many specialty stores. Some must order what you want; others have a large stock on hand.

—Warehouse showrooms: You'll probably pay less at these stores that specialize in a fast turnover and a cash-and-carry clientele. They stock everything more or less on the premises and thus avoid the enormously high overhead involved in custom ordering furnishings. Warehouse showrooms sell first-quality brand-new merchandise and should be distinguished from:

—Furniture clearance centers: Many department stores now have outlets where they sell their discontinued, returned, damaged, or out-of-season merchandise along with

Colorful contemporary prints and white paint work wonders with old furniture in this turn-of-the-century dining room. While curtains match chair upholstery, a completely different pattern appears on the walls.

items purchased expressly for the center. Again the prices are much lower, and the furnishings are immediately available.

Both warehouse showrooms and clearance centers are frequently located on major arteries in suburban areas. So there may be one near your country home.

—Mill outlet or remnant stores: These are often used by manufacturers to dispose of imperfect or discontinued merchandise. They are a particularly good source for fabric and carpeting.

Three different dining tables: *Top,
from left*, a Formica table in three
parts that can be moved apart and
rearranged; a roulette table (note
the *un*matching chairs); a tabletop
that was a door. *Right*, on one wall
of the living room, in full view of
the ocean, a distinctive dining area
with carved Venetian chairs
painted white, a plexiglass table,
and a Joseph Stella painting.

—Import stores: These stores sell smaller and less expensive furnishings from all over the world, such as Indian bedspreads and chairs made in Mexico.

—Five-and-tens, hardware stores, home improvement centers: Although these stores and others like them do not principally sell home furnishings, they do stock items for the home. For example, your local five-and-ten may have a good selection of lamps and curtains.

—Offbeat sources: An army supply store is the perfect place to buy extra cots for all those guests. The local cement company will probably have beautiful decorative cement blocks which can be grouped together to form small patio tables. And I recently bought some rag throw rugs at the A&P which I sewed together to make a large area rug.

—Homemade furniture: If you do not have the equipment, the skill, and the time, a nice man at a nearby lumberyard may oblige by cutting wood or plastic to size which you can then quickly "whip up" into your own furniture.

—Mail order: A large selection of good-quality merchandise is offered through mail-order companies. Certain things, like unfinished furniture, are available to residents of remote places only this way. The advantage of shopping by mail at seemingly reasonable prices may be offset by the length of time it takes for deliveries and the additional costs of handling and shipping.

Returning items to mail-order houses is fraught with hazards. To eliminate errors, read the descriptions carefully, including measurements, because pictures in catalogues can often be misleading. Write clearly. Be very precise in filling out the order blank.

Judging Quality

(The following can be applied also to secondhand furniture):

Examine all furnishings in a good light, from top to bot-

Modern furnishings, wood and sea-grass chairs on a woven cotton rug and around a plastic table, blend well with and update this East Hampton sun porch built in 1906.

tom and underneath. To check for structural soundness in a case piece, a chest of drawers, or a cabinet, push and pull it, see if the joints creak, if the drawers and doors open and close easily and smoothly.

A good-quality case piece will have fine hardware, a smooth, evenly matched finish; center or side guides and dovetailing on drawers, and reinforcing blocks in corners underneath.

Test an upholstered piece first for comfort and sturdiness. Although you cannot see its inner construction, certain clues on the outside will tip you off about the quality of the workmanship inside. If the piece is covered with a patterned fabric, the pattern should be centered and lined up from back to cushion and should be matched at the seams. The welting should lie straight, and both welting and stitching should be secure. Lift up the cushion, and feel the webbing below to make sure it is firm; the kind of filling used in the cushion will be indicated on a cushion label.

DIFFERENT MATERIALS

While most furniture is made of wood, there are many other materials available. In the tropics, where wood rot is a problem, many home owners substitute rattan (see p.189, "Outdoor Furniture"), plastic or plastic laminate, or furniture made from marine plywood.

Plastic furniture may be manufactured to look like itself or disguised as wood. While this material is extremely easy to clean and generally holds up very well, it does scratch. Clear plastic shows dust and unlike wood, which can be refinished, plastic cannot. Inflatable vinyl furniture can be easily punctured, and air can leak out of its seams.

Some metal furniture with a shiny finish such as chrome is impractical where moisture is present, and unless it is protected by a finish, it requires constant maintenance and waxing to prevent corrosion.

At right, folding, partially louvered doors, were added to the original stall space of this carriage house to make a living/sleeping area. Beds are covered with colorful throws and pillows, and between them a versatile wicker trunk is a combination desk/night table and storage piece.

In the carriage house shown below, with furniture of the Victorian era, the original door can be seen at the rear of the room.

Shopping and Ordering Long Distance

Certain precautions can help reduce mistakes:

—Try to get samples whenever possible of floor or wall coverings and fabrics. If, as is often the case, the store or manufacturer cannot supply them, then buy a small piece, such as a yard of fabric or a single floor tile. You should not only try the sample in your house but take it with you when shopping for other furnishings. Samples can also be used to test for quality. You can wash a fabric sample or leave it in bright sunlight to test colorfastness or grind food into the kitchen carpet tile to test stain resistance.

—If you are ordering merchandise, check availability and delivery time. Make sure that it is in stock, in the retailer's warehouse, not the manufacturer's factory, in the right size, number, and color. Get a firm delivery date.

—All orders should list a description of the merchandise, the color, the finish, the style or model number, the quantity, the price and, in addition, extras such as shelves, locks, casters, special finishes, plus delivery and crating charges.

—Keep sales slips, warranties, and do not be inhibited about complaining if you are sent a green couch instead of a yellow one. Although returning furniture under the best circumstances is frustrating, a reputable store will make good and sometimes even send their representative to remote islands to do so.

—If you are buying imperfect merchandise, make sure that the imperfection will not affect the overall appearance or wear; for example, a scratch on the rear leg of a couch set against the wall may not be visible. If you are buying discontinued merchandise, make sure that you have enough; if you are caught short on wallpaper or dishes, your great buy will be only a great lesson.

Making the Most of Old Furniture

If you are furnishing a country home, you'll probably find that old or secondhand furniture is more plentiful than new —either through the generosity of friends and relatives or through local sources. In some areas, it may be the only

Canopied bed, curtains that match, Louis XV chairs, an elaborate mirror, ceramic tile floor, and folding doors that open onto a balcony are the ingredients of this truly restful retreat.

Opposite, *top*, bedroom furniture built with the house and beds covered with quilted bed sheets. *Above*, furnishings for a little girl: hooked rugs, delicately shaped chest, and flowered cotton fabric on window, bed, and headboard. *Below*, the original stall of a restored barn is now a cozy bedroom. Stall hangings are Peruvian textiles.

available furniture. What you do with it is a good test of your ingenuity. If you're the least bit handy, it is easier than you think to rejuvenate. See p.224, "Do It Yourself," for more ideas.

Old pieces can be more interesting and, with the exception of good-quality antiques, will be much less expensive than new furniture. Some dealers in secondhand merchandise and antiques will permit you to try an item on approval before buying. Prices are generally subject to negotiation. Again, a few cardinal rules when using old furniture, whether an antique or a hand-me-down from your own home:

—Be adventuresome and open to the possibilities of utilizing the piece in a different, new way. Change it by removing old hardware or legs and adding new. Hang it on the wall upside down or even sideways. A breakfront intended for use in a dining room can make an excellent storage piece for a bedroom.

—In considering price, do not overlook the extra costs of cleaning, restoration, and delivery.

—Determine the degree of restoration required. Push, pull, and generally follow the guideline on p.104 for inspecting new furniture. Wear may be superficial, and a good cleaning may be all that is needed. On the other hand, if an upholstered piece cannot be renewed with cleaning and needs new covering at the least and possibly a complete overhaul of its innards at most, it may not be worth a second glance and the cost of a professional upholsterer. But then again it might be. If an upholstered piece is structurally sound, it can be covered quite inexpensively with a pretty blanket or a ready-made slip cover or a throw made of fabric (see p.230,"Do It Yourself").

Finding It

—Your own home and friends': Furnishings that you may

Junkyard "find": a wonderful old gate that now separates bedroom wing from the rest of the house.

be ready to discard in your city home may be given a new lease on life in your country home; similarly ask friends and family what they may have stored away in their attics. Offer to trade.

—In secondhand stores or junk shops.

—In merchandise offerings: Look at classified advertisements in papers in both town or country. If a telephone number is given, call first and try to get as much specific information in advance as possible and if you are serious, be the first one there. Look also at advertisements in antique journals. Put an ad in yourself for specific furnishings, for example: "Wanted—one couch."

—In thrift shops: By selling donated merchandise, which often includes good-quality home furnishings, a charitable organization, like the Salvation Army, can get extra funds. While the prices at thrift shops seem to be skyrocketing,

Making the most of old furniture: *Top left*, an infant's chest "aged" by adding new moldings and hardware. *Top right*, perpendicular to wall, bookcase becomes part night table, part desk.

Below, ends of a dining table sliced off to make two sideboards (one shown).

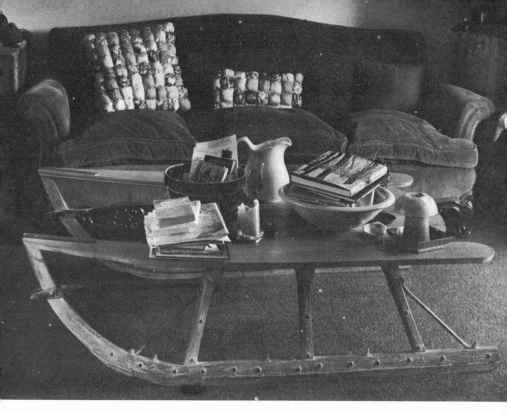

Above, a sled is a coffee table; butcher blocks are end tables.
Below, ceramic tiles glued to a tabletop.

they are still a major source and a good way to help the needy and yourself. Befriend the manager of the shop, so he'll tip you off when new shipments arrive.

—At church bazaars and hospital auctions: In smaller towns, instead of a thrift shop, a local charitable organization may run one-day events at which secondhand furnishings are sold. Because they are of a short duration and everything must go quickly, merchandise is priced to sell.

—At flea markets and antique shows: The quality at these vary widely. Some benefit a charity, others are run by professional organizations, and some are amateur efforts. Usually a lot of fun, especially on a nice day in the country, and a great challenge.

—At tag, garage, attic, and yard sales: All essentially the same—the name is derived from the location of the sale or the fact that the merchandise is tagged. Estates may be disposed of in this way. Often fascinating. An afternoon's entertainment. A look into someone else's life-style. In addition to home furnishings, the merchandise sold here can range from old love letters to shoes. See p. 80 for how to have your own yard sale.

—At wrecking companies: Not only a good source of secondhand building materials but decorative items, such as chandeliers, stained glass windows, or an interesting architectural member that could become the base of a table. Wrecking companies may have their own stores, or they may sell directly from a house that is being demolished. The contents of the house as well as its structural parts may be for sale.

Antiques

Antiquing for fun and to furnish is one popular vacation activity with a purpose. In the country what is called an antique is really something old with a lot of character. No one pays too much attention to age. A true "antique" is usually at least 100 years old or a newer piece with cultural or historical significance.

Practical considerations are important. Old furniture can often cost less and be better made and more interesting than new furniture. However, chairs that are delicate, chests with drawers that are too shallow to provide storage, and cabinets that require constant waxing may be right for a museum, but not for a functional home.

In addition to antique shops, antiques can be bought at many of the same places listed on p.112 for old furniture.

Cost and Value

While antiques can be modest in cost, in some resort areas at the height of the season they can be "otherworldly." To avoid being taken, especially if you are buying good-quality antiques and paying the price, protect your investment by finding out as much as possible about authenticity and value. If you are buying in town from a trustworthy dealer, then he should stand behind the purchase and give you a paper authenticating it; if you are buying out of town, you may be lucky enough to find an expert from a local museum, college, or restoration. If you are on your own, here are a few things to watch out for:

To determine how old a piece is, first, of course, look for any signs, signatures, or marks that might indicate age. Then examine it for evidence of hand carving and hand tools, such as planes. Chair rungs and table edges will be worn, and the dovetailing will be cruder and more uneven in an older piece. Generally, old-age shows. The piece will have the color or what the experts call the patina of age. Sometimes the story behind the piece, if believable, can help establish its age. To determine the condition of the piece, push and pull again and examine it in a good light (carry a flash light along), preferably outdoors in daylight. Look underneath. See if the piece has been restored. Has new hardware been added? Is it reconstructed, a new top been placed on an old base? If the piece requires refinishing or re-covering, add on what that will cost. Naturally, if you can do it yourself (see p.224), then you can often buy very well.

To evaluate the design, look at the lines of the piece, the color of the wood, the quality of the finish, and any special decorations like carving.

If the antique dealer does not have what you are looking for, he may be able to find it for you, so make a friend of him and tell him your needs. He may also be willing to sell on consignment or to trade furniture that came with your house.

BUYING ANTIQUES FOR LESS

Part of the challenge of antiquing is bargaining. Almost universally, if you say you are a dealer or a designer or indicate you are potentially the best customer ever or just plead poverty, you can get 10 percent knocked off the price. A quick cash-and-carry deal or the discovery of an imperfection—it is in poor condition, needs repairs or refinishing, or is of questionable age—can similarly reduce the price.

Auctions

Auctioning is like antiquing with all the challenge of discovery but easier on the feet. It's a good show and a good education in furniture styles and prices. All the ground rules for judging quality mentioned before should be religiously observed here. Everything is sold "as is," and dealers have been known to enter their worst junk in an auction just to get rid of it. There is every manner of auction from the formal sit-down variety with printed program and numbered merchandise to the casual walk-around kind where you pick out the merchandise and the auctioneer then auctions it off. At larger galleries, auction dates are announced

through notices in the mail and in newspapers. In smaller towns, notices may be posted on walls and in grocery stores. Most auctions are cash-and-carry, which means that you must put down at least 25 percent when you bid, the balance when you claim the piece, which is usually the same day or the next day. And you must carry—that is, you must remove or make arrangements to remove your purchase immediately. (For this reason, large bulky pieces of furniture can be cheap at auctions.)

Transportation may be a problem and an additional cost if you have bought many items or large ones that must go a distance to your home. I learned this from experience. My husband and I bought several pieces of furniture one winter Saturday at a New York auction gallery. If the merchandise had not been removed by the following Monday, we would have had to pay both storage charges (which is how I think the auction gallery makes its real money), and the moving fee to the storage place. We could have hired the movers (and there are usually many soliciting business at auctions) to bring everything to our New York apartment and then spent the rest of the winter figuring out how to get it to the country. However, we took the chairs by the seat, so to speak, and decided to rent a truck, pick up our purchases, and drive directly to the country.

Since the truck rental place closed before we got down there on Saturday, and the auction gallery was closed on Sunday, our only alternative was to move on Monday. My husband luckily had only five appointments on Monday, which he canceled, sheepishly muttering something about truck driving. Notwithstanding the snow and the unheated truck with a shift and the fact that we had to take a special truck route out and that there was no strong man at the other end to help us, we somehow made it. We were so numb by the time we got back that the fact our car had been towed away from in front of the truck rental office hardly made an impression. I must add that I love what I bought at that auction, and today, years after, I cherish it with an emotion that comes only as a result of a special kind of involvement.

Auctions are not always a free-for-all at which any price will do. Furnishings are frequently sold with a reserve, which means they cannot be sold for less than a previously determined amount. This is not dishonest—just a little misleading. It is done at some of the finest auction houses in the country. On the other hand, if the auction is for charity or for an estate, there may be no reserves, since the whole purpose is to sell everything at *any* price. A friend of mine. bought a wonderful sideboard this summer at one of these. It was $5, which is why, I think, she bought it. She didn't need it and is still trying to get rid of it.

Many dealers have told me that auctions are like buying at retail with entertainment and, sometimes, lunch thrown in. I know one auction house in a resort community that makes regular buying trips to New York antique dealers. Obviously they have to run their auction in such a way that they make a profit after the cost of the furniture and trucking and handling.

With care, education, and experience you cannot get hurt, even by a dishonest operation.

—First, examine everything fully before bidding. Measure it. Decide ahead of time whether the piece will fit in the house and will be the right size for the room. Determine if a chair is comfortable. How old is the piece in question, and if it is not in good condition, can it be easily repaired? Buy anything that you have seen for the first time on the auction block with the knowledge that you are gambling with poor odds.

—Establish the maximum price you will pay. Have confidence in your own decision, and do not be frightened off by the presence of dealers (this may only confirm the value of the piece). They generally cannot afford to pay as much as you can since they are buying for resale. Stick to this predetermined amount no matter how enticing the auctioneer (that is his job) or how badly you hate to lose.

Found furniture—tables: *Clockwise, from top* vinyl tacked over piece of wood on top of the from a broken table; a glass-covered cage; a sl marble on two cement blocks; a barrel; a tray column stage prop; a tree stump; table bases the milkman—a metal can and plastic box (not tin-can planters).

—Read the conditions of sale. This will tell you how much cash you must have with you and how much time you will be permitted to remove purchases. You will also probably find that the auctioneer or auction gallery is not responsible for the condition of lots (each piece auctioned) or the authenticity of a piece—no matter how it is described in the catalogue. At most auction galleries everything is final sale. But I have discovered that this can be negotiated. If you have misbought, sometimes the auctioneer will resell merchandise for you at a slight cost.

—Keep calm. When your number comes up, stand in the back so you can see where and who the competition is, and do not rush in at the first bid. As a matter of fact, you can enter the bidding at the end. Naturally the auctioneer will try to open or begin the bidding at the highest figure he can. However, if he gets no response, he will lower that figure until he does, assuming there is no reserve. Often someone in the audience will call out a figure. Once begun, bids move up in a set progression from, for example, $5–$10–$15–$20–$50–$100, etc. If the bidding quiets down and there seems to be no further interest, you can sometimes offer your own next price.

Found Furniture

There are a great many sources for things that can be converted into useful furnishings all around—in nature, behind stores, at the town dump. Not only are these things free, but they offer the opportunity to take advantage of the surroundings and to make a new creation from something that would otherwise have been wasted. For example, after a storm the beach can produce beautiful driftwood potentially for a future table, wall decoration, or lamp. Shells can be used as shade pulls or to trim an old mirror. A walk in the woods may produce a tree stump which when varnished can become a side table. An abundance of pine cones, sprayed with colored enamel, can be used as a table decoration.

Just think what you can do with tires, free for the taking at the local garage or tire store. Make a swing or a sandbox out of them; use them as bumpers on a dock and to hold garbage cans upright. And cable spools found behind electrical supply stores can be transformed into tables.

In one beach community the custom is to put discarded furniture in front of your house for any needy neighbors to cart away. There is a true story of one man who found a marvelous couch this way, hastily struggled to get it home, maneuvered it with difficulty upstairs, only to find when he turned it upside down that it was the very couch, now recovered, that he had thrown away five years before.

Town dumps used to be a remarkable source of furniture, but I am now told that in some places only those with permits—whom I assume to be junk dealers—are allowed to scavenge. However, city streets are still fair game; if you know what day furniture pickups are made by the sanitation department, get there before they do. Some surprisingly good furniture is discarded, particularly in affluent areas.

The possibilities inherent in a wooden crate—a seat with cushion, a table, stacked to be a bookcase—are restricted only by the limits of your imagination. And you don't have to worry if it decays or blows out to sea in a hurricane; you can just go down to the grocery store and replace it.

That is the fun and challenge of found furniture.

Moving and Deliveries

It costs $1 to take a box of groceries on the Fire Island ferry (there are few stores and no cars on the island), but it doesn't cost anything to get a couch there—if you buy from the right store. Moving furnishings to country homes is not as simple as it seems. To keep costs down and deliveries smooth, plan ahead.

Shopping

Buy what is not only ready but compact. Furnishings that are knocked down (KD) or come apart, deflate, roll up, or come in sections (called modules) are more portable—not only easier for you to move but cheaper if commercially delivered. As mentioned before, be sure that what you are buying or being given is what you want, will fit, and is not falling apart and, if it comes in parts, that you will know how to put it together.

Do It Yourself

For anyone who is going to furnish a new home from antique shops, auctions, and other local sources, a basic piece of equipment is a large station wagon, fully equipped with a rack on top and a dolly inside, a lot of ropes, and some old blankets. You could borrow or rent one if you have only an occasional move to make.

You can, also, rent a small truck, or a U-Haul, which is attached to the back of your car. Find out how much these will hold, whether you can leave the truck or U-Haul at a drop-off point near your home, if you are restricted from certain highways, and how much the rental will cost.

Consider how much moving in and out of houses and stores is involved before you go ahead and commit yourself to doing it alone.

Professional Movers

You can hire a moving company to move a houseful of furniture or just a few pieces that you'd like to transport from one home to another. Get estimates from movers both in the country and in town. It is sometimes cheaper to have a country mover come to town, and the service is often more personal. Big-city movers usually require full payment in cash on delivery. And if you do not have enough money, which can easily happen since their estimates are often much too low, you could find them carting your furniture back off to town until you paid. Country movers are more trusting. Whomever you hire, be ready when he comes; that means have anything that is being moved dismantled and disconnected. Make arrangements for someone to be at the other end—someone other than the previous owner who may not have moved out yet!

Store Delivery and Sales Tax

More than likely you will, at some point, buy something in a store that will have to be delivered to your house. The charges and methods of shipping vary greatly, not only from one area to another, but from one store to another. So it's a good idea to do some research in advance, and in some cases you may want to pick your store before you select your furniture. For example, if you buy from department store X, delivery to your out-of-state house may be free because it has a branch store near it. But the same store may charge you sales tax, whereas one without a local branch store may not. Policies about purchases sent as gifts also vary. In my research for this book, I discovered that some stores will suggest to the customer that he save sales tax by sending the purchase to the country home as a gift. Others will exempt gifts from sales tax only when sent to persons outside the household. The general attitude of most salespeople toward the sales tax on out-of-state shipments is one of great confusion. Since tax on furnishings as well as delivery charges can really add up, the only safe course is to check the policy of the store before buying.

Where you must bear the cost of delivery, do not assume that expense will be based strictly on distance. Alternative methods of shipment may make it less expensive to send your purchase a longer distance.

Here are some representative figures from a major department store based on shipping two beds (box springs and mattresses):

To St. Croix by air cargo: $40—no sales tax.

To Vermont by store truck: $55.00—no sales tax.

To Fire Island: no delivery charge, but sales tax.

Delivery charges usually include handling and insurance (but not crating) and are dependent on the weight, volume, value, and method of transportation—Railway Express, parcel post, air cargo, United Parcel, etc. Air cargo has tried to keep its rates low and competitive. That is why it is cheaper to send all but a big load abroad air cargo rather than ocean freight, where the minimum cost is $85.

TERMS YOU SHOULD KNOW

—*F.O.B.:* means "freight on board." What it means to you is more money. Delivery charges extra.

—*C.O.D.:* You pay the cost of the item (cash on delivery).

—*Express collect:* You pay the delivery charges when the item is delivered.

—*Drop delivery:* Your purchase is delivered and literally dropped some place, not in your living room, sometimes in the middle of the street (sidewalk delivery), possibly in the next town.

ARRANGING FOR DELIVERIES

Always get a delivery date when you make a major purchase. The store may have to check with the manufacturer, the warehouse, or the carrier, but you should pin it down. It is even possible to get the exact flight of an air cargo delivery if you are persistent. Not only is it nice to know when you can begin using your furniture, but it's essential for the owner of a second home to know the date so that arrangements can be made for someone to receive it.

If possible, you should be at the other end on delivery day. Then you can check to be sure the merchandise is what you ordered, that it is in good condition, that it is placed in the right room, and that cumbersome wrapping is removed. If something is wrong, you can give the merchandise right back to the delivery man and thus avoid the hassle of returning it to the store later on. If you cannot be there, the following alternative arrangements can be made:

—Tell the driver to ring the bell of a neighbor who has a key (make sure *he* will be home).

—Pay your baby-sitter, house watcher, or other local person to be there that day.

—Leave a cellar or garage door open, and indicate on the order that the driver should leave it there.

—Make arrangements with a local store to leave your purchase there until you arrive. (Better warn them if you will not arrive for several months.)

—Make arrangements with a moving and storage company to leave purchase there. It makes sense to leave new furniture that is being delivered to a house in construction at a local moving and storage company until the house is in move-in condition.

If someone is not there, this is what can happen:

A couch is ordered from a large department store, and it is delivered two weeks early—a historic moment in the furniture industry where few things come on time. No one is home because the house is semiclosed for the winter. The couch is left on the open, exposed, cold, snowy breezeway and sits there until the owner arrives two weeks later on what was supposed to be the delivery day. Now it is necessary to call in a local mover to move it first to the upholsterer, so that the damaged covering can be replaced, and then back into the house.

Three patterns that work well together; a horizontal stripe at the window, a vertical stripe on the wall, and a plaid on the bed. Cushions on toy chests make more seating.

CHAPTER FIVE

PAINT, FABRIC, AND COUNTRY COLORS

Miracle workers for any house, and especially a country home, paint and fabric are the most effective, yet least expensive way to introduce color and pattern into a room.

Color Schemes

There seem to be two basic schools of thought on the subject of using color in a home in the country. One is that colors should be played down and made to complement God's colors, so that together with the use of natural materials the house becomes an extension of the outdoors. In homes with a great deal of glass or in rooms with large picture windows this makes sense. The colors of flowers, trees, the sky, patios, and decks all become part of your decorating scheme. The inside and the outside are one.

The other faction says bring color in. A garden of gay fabrics can be very cheerful in a house that does not have many windows, one that is closed in. And certainly color can do much to warm a winter house or a house in a cold climate where the colors outside are bleak and gray.

The psychological impact of a color is an important consideration. In a cool climate warm colors may make you feel warmer, and in warm climates cool colors may make you feel cooler. Some people have a preference for monotone colors or, conversely, very bright palettes wherever they may be and whatever the weather.

Another factor is the style and condition of the house. In a brand-new beautiful modern house, with fantastic materials and lovely lines, color may play less of a role. Alternatively, the introduction of yards of a dashing chintz, together with bright paint on walls, floors, and ceilings, can magically transform an old wreck of a house that is in need of instant and inexpensive remodeling. The same is true of furniture. A new well-designed piece can stand on its own, but an older one might need some cosmetics, a fresh coat of paint, or a new seat cover.

White, particularly in a warm climate, can be cooling when used alone and very crisp and vivid when used in combination with one or more colors. White with neutral colors will make the neutrals seem to come alive and bring out the color in them. White seems to contain and calm very bright colors. When used in small amounts, dotted around the room, white (and black, also) can add a sharp note to any color scheme.

Guaranteed to inhibit even the most daring, the choice of a color scheme is often the greatest stumbling block in decorating. Yet colors and color schemes are really not picked out of the air at random. There usually is some point of departure, such as the climate, the colors in the garden, or the color of the house itself. A special painting or picture, an area rug, a wallpaper, or fabric pattern—all could suggest a color scheme. If you are decorating a bedroom, perhaps you should select the bedspreads or curtains first and develop your color scheme from the colors in them. It's hard to make a mistake by borrowing from a professional colorist/designer who is trained to put colors together.

If the house is carpeted, the color scheme might be planned around this color. But never plan around furnishings, couch, draperies or floor coverings that you dislike or that will soon fall apart.

Walls, floors, and ceilings are the largest areas in a room

to be decorated, and the strongest color statement is made here. Couch, bedcover, window treatment, and lounge chair are considered medium-size color areas, and smaller accents of color can be found on occasional chairs, pillows, lamps, picture and furniture frames. If, for argument's sake, you are decorating a bedroom working around the colors red, white, and blue in a curtain, your color scheme might be as follows: red walls, white floor covering and ceiling, blue bedcovering, blue chair with red painted frame, white lamps, and red and white pillows on the bed.

A feeling of cohesiveness and spaciousness is achieved when a few colors that are related are used throughout the inside and outside of a house. A further dividend is greater flexibility in furniture arrangement—you can rearrange or move furniture about from one area to another while maintaining the color scheme. For example, to carry the red, white, and blue scheme further, one room might be predominantly blue with other tones of blue and white, another room might be predominantly white with blue and red accents. The floor color throughout could be white, the color of the house itself, white with red shutters and doors and flowers red, white, and blue. This is a gross simplification meant to illustrate a point only and does not take into account different color values, patterns, and textures.

When matching colors of furnishings, it is best to select the color of the floor covering, such as carpeting, first because the choice will be limited, then the fabric or wall covering and last, the paint, which can always be custom mixed to match.

Effects with Paint

Paint can be used to give color and new life to walls, furniture, picture frames, lamps, even upholstery, just about anything in sight:

—For interesting effects on the walls, paint large strips or squares of paint in different colors. Do a large freehand

Above, moldings on
around door and basebo
are highlighted.

Effects with paint: *Above, left*, each panel of a folding door and each door down
a hall are painted in different colors. *Center*, on walls and ceilings, moldings painted
a contrasting color. *Bottom*, a geometric design of triangles, scallops, and stripes
painted all over.

swirling design. Paint all moldings—doors, windows, base-boards—a contrasting color (for the less steady-handed put colored tape on molding instead). Stencil the wall.

—Different textures can be achieved with paint. A high-gloss enamel paint or any paint covered with a glossy varnish can simulate shiny vinyl; a textured paint or any paint mixed with sand or crumpled shells can simulate rough stucco.

—Paint in a dark color can look like paneling, at a fraction of the cost.

—Remodel with paint which can be used to create certain visual effects. If a radiator is painted the same color as the wall behind it, it will almost disappear; if it is painted a contrasting color, it will jump out at you. If a ceiling is too high, paint it a color. This will have the visual effect of lowering it—the ceiling will seem to advance. If the ceiling is low, it should be painted white or a very light receding color to make it seem higher. Similarly, by making the short wall come forward through the use of color, a long, skinny room will appear to be wider.

Wide bands of color applied to walls horizontally will "break" the height of the wall and make the same walls appear shorter and the ceiling lower. Wallpaper and fabric can be utilized in a similar manner—on the ceiling only to lower it, vertical stripes on one wall to heighten it. Wall-paper applied horizontally only to the bottom part of a wall would tend to widen a wall and make it lower.

For more ideas on how to use paint and color and what kind of paint to buy, see p.232,"Do It Yourself."

How to Use Fabric and Pattern

Fabric too is a great disguiser and cover-up that can also be applied to almost anything—walls, ceiling, furniture, windows, bed, lampshades. Old furniture covered in a bright new fabric will be rejuvenated.

PATTERNS

The basic motif of the fabric should be related to the overall design theme of the area. If the furnishings are very modern, a classic floral chintz may not be appropriate, and a very modern fabric might not go on Victorian chairs. But then again it might—if you like the look. It is just a good idea to know the rules before breaking them.

The scale (size) and pattern of the fabric should be related to the piece it is covering. An oversized print might look ridiculous on an undersized chair, and geometric designs like plaids and stripes may look better on angular pieces than on curvy pieces. If the fabric is to go on a couch, it should not be seamed but run lengthwise or railroaded. Fabric should be installed upright with flowers and leaves growing in the right direction.

The texture and weight of the fabric should relate to its use. At windows it can be lightweight and either porous or opaque depending on how much light you want to shine through. On upholstery it should be heavier. While fabric that is on upholstery is usually cleaned or wiped off, fabric on the windows of a country home could be machine-washable.

The fabric should be easy to maintain. A fabric that has a water- and stain-resistant finish of Zepel or Scotchgard will be so labeled. Whenever possible, fabrics should be removable for washing or cleaning (fabric that is washable will also be so labeled). A light no-pattern fabric or a patterned fabric with a white background will, obviously, show dirt faster than a medium-toned fabric or one with a darker background color or a busy pattern. For fabric on outdoor furniture, see p.189.

The selection of fabrics should not be limited to those found in home furnishing departments. Investigate dress fabrics, especially the wide variety of cotton prints. Use colorful sheets, Indian bedspreads, antique pieces of fabric, samples, and remnants, or make your own fabric (see p.248).

On lounge chair and ottoman, window seat, stretched on rods on the walls, and at window (triple tied-back curtains let in more light), two patterns dominate, but several others appear on pillows.

Fabric from an old piece of clothing (clean, please) may be just right for the covering of a small chair.

More than one patterned fabric can be used in an area and with good results as long as the fabrics are related in color. To be on the safe side, the same two or three colors should be in all fabrics in the room, and one color may dominate. This works best if the patterns are different scale and design—for example, a small-scaled blue and white check with a large-scaled blue and white floral.

If the fabric has a pattern, the pattern should be matched. If the repeat is large, buy additional fabric to make up for fabric wasted in matching. Even a solid fabric has a subtle direction, and this should also be matched.

Construction

Fabrics are made of one or more (blend) of the following fibers:

Natural fibers: cotton, wool, silk, and linen.

Synthetic fibers: nylon, acrylic, Saran, polyester, polyolefin, glass, rayon, and acetate. Synthetic fibers do not mildew.

Basic weaves are pile, plain, satin, twill, and jacquard.

Fabric is made in widths ranging from 36 to 54 inches. A few, such as felt, are manufactured in 72-inch widths.

Upholstery

A fabric on permanently upholstered pieces, as opposed to chair seats which can be easily changed, will take a lot of wear and will be costly to replace. Therefore, upholstery fabric should be easy to clean and colorfast and sturdy. Pull it; feel how thick it is; hold it up to the light to see if it is closely woven. For extra "body" a lighter-weight fabric can be quilted.

However, a slip seat is easily re-covered (see p. 231 for how to) when necessary, so just about any fabric will do, even a lightweight cotton.

Fabric everywhere: Natural raw silk on U-shaped couch and library walls.

Fabric-filled bedrooms.

SLIP COVERS

These have been used as a summer covering for upholstered pieces, but now they are appropriate the year round.

Fabric for slip covers should be shrink-resistant if you plan to wash them. However, just to be on the safe side, you may want to dry clean slip covers. A large couch slip cover is really too cumbersome to wash at home anyway. Slip covers can be made of light but sturdy fabrics, such as cotton duck, denim, canvas (usually cotton or cotton and a synthetic blend).

If slip covers are made of upholstery-weight fabric, they will look more like upholstery than slipcovers. But make sure that the fabric is not too thick to be sewn. The advantage of slip covers over reupholstery is that they are less expensive, and the covers are changeable and removable for laundering. (See p.230, "Do It Yourself Slip Covers.")

CURTAINS, DRAPERIES, AND SHADES

The practical considerations here include how much light, if any, should filter through the fabric, whether the fabric is intended to insulate, whether it should be washable. A fabric that is going to be laminated to a shade must be fairly thin and tightly woven so that the shade is not too bulky. Sheet "fabric" is ideal. Washable curtains are a fine idea for a low-maintenance home, and if they are drip dry, so much the better. However, consider the size of the curtains if you plan to wash them. Not a problem with café curtains that can be tossed into a washing machine, but you would need a swimming pool to wash wall-to-wall curtains. Heavy fabric draperies are good insulators and might be the right choice for a ski house. Curtains or draperies may be lined with a tightly woven fabric like cotton sateen to protect against fading and sun rot, common in the country home. For more on this, read on.

Extra advice: If you need fabric to match a newly bought

sofa or chair, request extra yardage from the manufacturer or department store.

Often fabric from a decorator showroom can be bought at mill end, remnant, and discount stores. Frequently the fabric is perfect, a manufacturer's leftover or a return. If it is damaged, imperfect in color, weave, or pattern, but the imperfection is small or in an inconspicuous spot, it may be possible to disregard it or to cut it out. While fabric should always be examined before buying, it is crucial in this kind of store to go over it inch by inch.

Fading

In the fifteenth and sixteenth centuries, dyers were punished by death if their fabrics faded; it is a good thing for today's dyers that this practice is no longer followed. Fading is a problem that plagues many country homeowners whose homes are most exposed to the elements and often have a great deal of glass which reflects and magnifies the sun and snow.

Fading can occur as a result of many things: impurities in the air, perspiration, washing, or rubbing. The kind of fading the homeowner is most concerned with is fading from exposure to light and washing. What most people want to know is how to prejudge a fabric or carpet's ability to withstand fading. The problem is a complex one. There are few answers. No fabric is guaranteed against fading, but there are better risks. Most manufacturers test their fabrics or fibers for fading. The voluntary industry standard for lightfastness of fibers used for floor coverings is 80 hours, for draperies 60 hours, and for upholstery 40 hours. This means that materials should not fade in less than that number under laboratory conditions that simulate strong July sunlight at noon in Washington, D.C. Sixty hours, less than three days, seems a short time when you consider the number of hours curtains can hang in the direct and powerful sunlight. Since the standard appears to be low, the first answer seems to be to observe certain precautions:

Make sure curtains and draperies never turn to the sun and are protected from the direct rays of the sun at all times. This means they should be lined unless they are made of fiber glass, the fiber most highly resistant to fading. Special tinted window glass, a roof overhang, or awning can block the rays of the sun. Draw blinds or close curtains during peak hours of sun to protect floor and fabric covering in the room. This will also keep the house cool.

Lightfastness is a result of good dyes and the kind of fiber. A fiber that is solution-dyed (the fiber is actually spun from colored filament) will be very light-resistant. Some carpet manufacturers label a carpet that has been solution-dyed, but fabric manufactuers do not. Vat dyes are considered the best available dyes and, when they are used with cotton, produce a very light-resistant fabric, but this is not so labeled either. Bright colored dyes are supposed to hold best to acrylic fibers. Acetates hold dye poorly.

Although a fabric will fade in the wash, it may not necessarily fade at the window. Light and water fading are two different things.

Obviously if you start off with a fabric that has little or no color, like white, it will not fade.

Very large chain stores test their own fabrics for lightfastness and since they have more customers to please, their product may hold up better. If a fabric fades in an unusually short time, you can send it back to the store or manufacturer and they can have an unfaded section tested to see whether it was up to standard. But this offers small consolation to the person who has already paid to have the fabric made into a slip cover or curtain.

Backgrounds: natural wood walls, an Oriental rug, a bottoms-up window shade.

CHAPTER SIX

BACKGROUNDS

Windows

There are two good reasons for unadorned windows in a country home; the best window treatment is a beautiful view, and unnecessary window coverings are wasteful in both cost and maintenance. A house may have a built-in shield, deep roof overhangs which block the sun's rays, fences, or natural shrubbery for privacy, or it may be located in an isolated area.

On the other hand, people who live next to beach clubs shouldn't have glass houses. In many country homes, window coverings may be essential not only for privacy but for light control, for protection against fading, and for insulation. The amount of light is controlled by the degree of opacity of a window covering, whether it is opaque, translucent, or transparent; draperies help keep a room warm or cool.

A window treatment can be a decorating asset and the focal point of a room, even in a house that for practical reasons may not need one. While traditional swags and ruffles might be out of character in a very contemporary house, modern vertical blinds or drapery panels can go a long way to modernize an older one. And a lovely view may disappear at sunset, unless the exterior is illuminated, leaving only the inky blackness of night at a bare window.

The dimensions of a window can be remodeled with a well-planned window treatment, and an awkward window transformed into a thing of beauty. If a window is small and

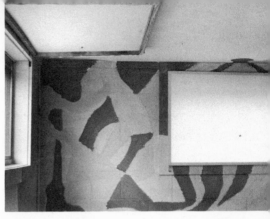

Top left, one way to install shutters when there no one handy in the country to help—have a professional in town fit them into a separate frame then nail the entire unit to the window frame *Top right*, the invention of the owner—stretch and staple fabric onto a wood frame the size of the window; hinge to top of window frame, hook to screw eyes in ceiling to open, to wall to close *Bottom*, for almost maximum light and privacy a panel of stained glass bought from a house wrecker.

insignificant, it can be covered with curtains in such a way that it will appear to be much larger. Adjacent windows of different sizes can be equalized or made to look like one, and windows lengthened or made wider depending on the placement of the rod, other hardware, and the cornice. For example, to make a window appear taller, hang a curtain from some point above the window frame, not on it; to widen, extend the rod beyond the side boundaries of the window. Apply the same concept to other window coverings such as shades and shutters.

It can be difficult and expensive to have a window treatment custom made in the country. Alternatives include making your own (see p. 242), buying made-to-measures (a hybrid between custom-made and ready-to-hang available in good department stores), or buying ready-mades. Most curtains or draperies are manufactured in standard lengths of 30, 36, 45, 54, 63, 72, 84, 90, 95, 99, 108 inches and pleated widths of 48 inches, one and a half widths of 72 inches, double widths of 96 inches and triple widths of 144 inches. Manipulate them to fit those odd-sized windows so often found in country homes as follows: To lengthen, add fringe or ribbon to the top or bottom of the curtain, or adjust, raise, or lower rods and rings or hooks. To widen, add fringe or ribbon to the sides. Ready-mades can look custom-made by sewing or glueing on decorative trim in colors coordinated with the room. Use white or fabric glue.

CURTAINS AND DRAPERIES

Curtains and draperies add softness and color to the window area. They should be made from a washable fabric unless they are so large that washing is impractical. Colored curtains that are exposed to harsh sun should be lined for colorfastness. Curtains can be hung wall to wall, on the frame or inside it, from ceiling to floor or to sill, and can be stationary, nonmoving, or moving. If they draw, decide which way, from center out, from right to left or left to right. Determine how much room the opened curtain will take. These considerations are particularly important when you plan a curtain that will cover a glass sliding door. Decide whether the hardware should be concealed or played up with the addition of fancy rods and rings.

Shades

Window shades are economical, easy to maintain, and clean-cut in appearance, and decorative shades are marvelous for a country home. Shades can be used alone or with curtains or other window treatments. Shades can be made of many materials, including cloth, plastic, wood, or bamboo. Usually installed on the top of the window either inside the frame or on it, they can also be installed on the bottom of the window and made to roll up. This allows light to come in at the top while shielding the view at the bottom. For complete light and privacy control shades are sometimes installed in the center of a window; one shade rolls up from the center, and the other rolls down. By switching the position of the hardware and the roller, a shade can be made to "reverse roll," which means it rolls in the opposite direction than usual. This gives a neater appearance at the top, particularly for a colored or patterned shade. The wrong or underside will not show.

Always consider the porosity of the shade and how much light will pass through it. If you like to sleep late, buy room-darkening shades.

When replacing a cloth shade, measure the window width and length carefully. Even better, if you have the old shade or at least the roller, take it to the store. Precise measurements are crucial. To the length of the window add 18 inches to allow for rolling up. If the roller is cut too narrow, sometimes you can pull the pin in the roller out a little bit, or buy special adjustable shade brackets that correct this error. Shades can also be customized and personalized by attaching various trims, including colored tapes, ribbons,

Above, simple but smart tie-back draperies, shades and valances trimmed in a color chosen from the couch fabric. *Below*, an Austrian shade pulls up and down but is more formal and softer in feeling than a conventional shade.

Top left: bordering a window covered w
matchstick shade, narrow shelves and a wi
seat that lifts up for storage. *Top right*, a sw
decorative rope with tassels hung up with
hooks. *Bottom left*, tiny windows enlarge
hanging two tiered café curtains, the upper
tain on the window, the lower curtain ove
wall. *Bottom right*, short curtains with tie
in a different fabric, adapting the two fabr
sign of the chair cushion.

and fringe. For how to cover shades with fabric or how to make your own, see p. 241.

OTHERS

Curtains, draperies, and shades are the most common kind of window covering, but there are many other kinds including:

—Shutters can be painted, stained, or covered with fabric or wallpaper. Painting the slats on louvered shutters can be agony although paint in a spray can will ease the pain; as an alternative, buy prepainted louvered shutters or unpainted shutters without louvers.

—Blinds are available in horizontal or vertical styles made of plastic or metal. Vertical blinds are also made of cloth. Blinds are sleek and contemporary in appearance and excellent for light and privacy control. They are quite easy to maintain, less of a dust collector out in the clean country air than in the city, and a very good choice for a leisure home. Blinds may be used alone or in combination with curtains or draperies.

—Panels of fabric can be hung from a special curtain rod that is made for this purpose. They are like sliding panels without wood or metal frames.

Walls

Just as a stage backdrop sets the scene for a show, the walls can establish the leitmotif of a decorating scheme: formal or informal, modern or traditional. Walls are the largest element of a room and, if played up with a strong color or pattern, the most dominant.

The treatment of the walls can affect the appearance of the size of a room. A horizontal pattern may reduce the height and a vertical pattern increase it. A bold color on walls will advance and make the area seem smaller and cozier, a good way to fill too large an area without furniture,

Problem windows: *Above*, vertical blinds on trapezoidal windows; *at right*, an awning window with three sashes covered with three tiny curtains; *top*, *right*, shutters.

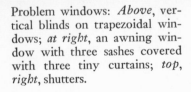

while the same walls in a soft and light color will recede and make the area seem larger.

Walls can be rough or smooth, rustic or finished, patterned or plain. In many country homes the loveliest and most carefree walls are of building materials, brick, wood, ceramic tile, cement or stone. Indeed, unmasking such a wall that has been covered can be very exciting. However, don't go around pulling down walls (and ceilings, or ripping up floors) without a clue that what is underneath is worth exposing.

Other building materials such as plaster and sheet rock should probably be covered or re-covered. Basic covering materials are paint, fabric, paneling, and wallpaper (not always paper—it can be vinyl or plastic or paper-backed fabric). But even traditional floor coverings such as carpet and resilient tiles, straw mats, and building materials like wood shingles or aluminum siding can cover walls.

The choice, if it has not been made already by the builder or the previous owner, may depend on what materials and labor are available. A ceramic tile wall should be professionally installed, but a self-adhesive plastic in a tile pattern can be an easy-to-apply substitute; similarly, paint requires less skill and is more readily available than paneling.

Paint

The easiest and least expensive wall "'covering" with the greatest versatility, paint comes in many finishes from flat to textured to high-gloss enamel and in unlimited colors. The days when semigloss or high gloss were banished to kitchen, bath, and woodwork are over, and these wonderfully washable finishes are practical and pretty on all the walls of a house. (For how to paint, see p.232,"Do It Yourself.")

Wallpaper

There is nothing that can dress up a room and furnish it

quite like wallpaper. Available in a multitude of patterns, colors, and textures, a washable paper which is supposed to last longer than paint is a wise choice for a country home. A vinyl with a cloth back is a particularly good covering for old cracking walls. Prepasted paper is advertised as being easier to apply, though in truth this appears to be a moot point. But pretrimmed and strippable paper is definitely geared to the do-it-yourselfer. Self-adhesive plastic (Con-Tact) which bubbles and sticks to itself when applied to a flat surface is a snap to put on walls.

Wallpaper can be applied to all walls or just one or two, a ceiling, in alternating strips of wallpaper and bare wall, or horizontally in dado fashion. Using what is on hand, wallpaper can be made from magazine covers, gift or brown wrapping paper, comics, newspapers, family photographs, just about anything that can go on with white glue. Not only can you use different materials as "wallpaper," but you can cover accessories, furniture and floors with it. To protect a homemade wallpaper or a nonwashable paper cover it with polyurethane. For how to wallpaper, see p.234, "Do It Yourself."

FABRIC

Fabric is a versatile wall covering especially good for the older house whose aging walls are not young enough for a smooth paint or paper job. And fabric has several other advantages. It insulates and deadens sound. It has a warm appearance. Gay, inexpensive cotton prints including bed sheets and dress fabric are often more plentiful than wallpaper. There is almost always an outlet in the country for fabric, including the five-and-ten and general store, but not always for wallpaper. Also, the same fabric can cover chairs, pillows, tables, and windows and even be draped from the ceiling—rich effects that belie their low cost. Fabric that has been stapled on or attached with double-faced tape can

An extra service performed by one winter's house watcher: She
painted this jungle scene on the wall of the nursery.

be removed and used again, and staple holes normally will not show.

Fabric installation is a do-it-yourself job. Not just by default because it is hard to find a professional to put fabric up but also because it requires less precision than wallpaper. Fabric can be easily attached to the wall with white glue, staples, tacks, or double-faced tape. It can also be laminated professionally to a paper backing and then applied like wallpaper or shirred on rods that are hung at or near the ceiling and floor.

Fabric walls are impractical where excess dirt or moisture are likely to be present, such as in a kitchen, playroom, or bathroom. For how to install a fabric wall, see p.237, "Do It Yourself."

PANELING

Good insulators, hardy, easy to care for, rich in appearance and sound-deadening. If you are not lucky enough to have natural wood interior walls that are a part of the original structure of the house, you can buy a wide variety of wood paneling unfinished or factory-finished. These include plywood with a real wood veneer (most expensive) or hardboard with a printed-on pattern that looks like wood but is less costly. Other kinds of paneling include a decorative variety of unfinished hardboard which is more frequently used as a window covering or room divider than as a wall covering, pegboard used for wall or closet storage, plastic laminate imitations of marble, wood, and ceramic tile, and vinyl-covered gypsum.

CERAMIC TILE

Expensive to buy and to install. It is easy to clean and impervious to everything. For these reasons, it is used principally on kitchen and bathroom walls. Ceramic tile is avail-

Kinds of walls: *Above left*, brick behind bathtub is the other side of the living room fireplace. *At right*, decorative ceramic tile on wall as well as tabletop. *Below left*, sisal covers walls and bench of a bathhouse (shelf is driftwood). *Below right*, wood walls of pecky cyprus.

Top left, wallpaper on only one wall played off against painted walls makes stronger statement than if it had been used all over. *Right,* wallpaper glued onto panels in door. *Below,* paint in a bright red contrasts with white wicker furniture, doors, and curtains.

Wallpaper in the kitchen: *Top left*, kitchen cabinets covered, as well as walls. *Right*, a fabulous fake that looks like cork; *bottom*, checks— a charming background for unusual accessories, including a wire chicken basket and an old English railroad lantern.

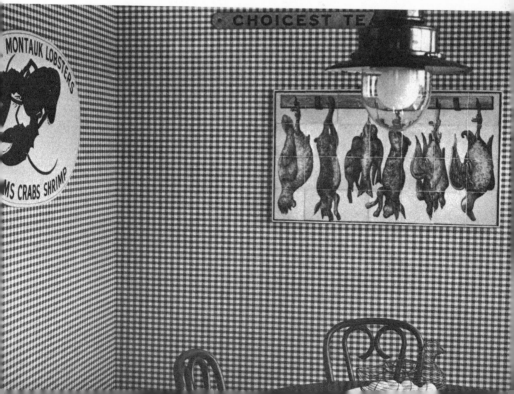

Different ways with wallpaper: Wallpaper that matches roman window shade is applied half way up the wall to dado.

Wallpaper on ceiling matches fabric on table, but for variety, chair cushions and sofa are upholstered in a different but compatible print.

Ceilings—bottles, blankets, and fabric: *Top*, bottles and fishing equipment; *Center*, assorted blankets, carpets, and bed throws tacked and draped from ceiling; *bottom*, fabric gathered on rods is stretched across ceiling. Fabric also covers curtain rods and the chains on poolroom light fixtures.

able glazed or unglazed in a glossy or mat finish and in a variety of colors, patterns, and shapes.

IMITATIONS

There are all manner of fakes now on the do-it-yourself market—plastic or metal tiles, some with adhesive backs that resemble and can often be used in place of ceramic tile, and fiber glass bricks that are hard to distinguish from real ones, lighter and easier for the amateur to install.

Floors

A great floor can make or break the appearance of a room, whether it is an inexpensive homemade paint and stencil job or a professionally installed costly ceramic tile floor. It can also break the bank and—taking care of it—your back.

One continuous floor material wall to wall and room to room conveys a feeling of space and serenity; several rugs and changes of floor surface visually divide space and make too large an area appear smaller.

While it is nice to have something lovely to look down at, for the leisure homeowner the biggest consideration after, if not before, appearance is maintenance. If you ask a lot of people what floor material is easiest to take care of, you will get a lot of different answers. To some, using carpet, rug, a resilient floor covering, or a floor of natural materials, such as wood or brick, is a question of whether you prefer to mop, vacuum, sweep, or hose down. The amount of necessary cleaning can be sharply reduced with the right floor, and waxing and polishing can be completely eliminated.

The best floor for a country home should wear well and be easy to maintain, hide dirt, and, where applicable, camouflage sand and absorb snow. Depending on the climate, it should feel warm or cool underfoot, and it should not rot, crack or otherwise deteriorate owing to extremes in temperature in a house that is closed down part of the year or as the result of dampness.

The condition of your present floor and the availability of sources of both supply and labor may narrow the choice. If there is no floor finisher or tile layer for miles and the nearest carpet store closed down five years ago, obviously the options are reduced. Then the only solution might be do-it-yourself vinyl tiles or a good floor polish or some nice old rugs brought up from town.

CARPETS AND RUGS

—Carpets and rugs are warm-feeling and sound-deadening and insulate against cold.

—Wall-to-wall carpeting (broadloom), unless it is of the do-it-yourself variety and you are willing to, requires professional installation and, if you're fussy, professional cleaning. A large area rug, almost wall to wall, does not require either.

—Carpets and rugs can be laid to rest over a floor that has seen better days, but when a resilient floor is put down, the underfloor must be in good condition.

—Depending on color and weave, carpets and rugs may not show dirt as quickly as a hard-surface floor.

—A small rug called an area rug because it defines an area of the floor such as a seating complex in front of a fireplace can add great decorating interest. Some area rugs are so attractive that they can be, and often are, hung on the wall.

—The selection is greater for a country home where novelty rugs—such as cotton, plastic, and straw—fit a casual life-style. Many of these are so inexpensive that they are sometimes worth buying for temporary use in a rented house.

—Although there is no such thing as a secondhand tile floor, secondhand rugs are plentiful. They can probably be

Border of custom-made area rug repeats drapery border.

bought at stores and auctions in your area, as well as in town.

—Rugs do have a way of moving about, and if this happens, they should be put in their place with carpet tape. This is tape that has adhesive on both sides.

—Unless the rug or carpet covers almost the entire floor, some attention may have to be paid to refinishing or otherwise renewing the part of the floor left showing. This is not necessary with wall-to-wall carpeting, which hides the floor beneath.

—In many cases a carpet store, even one that is far away, will arrange to have its own staff or someone it knows in the area measure and install the carpet you have purchased. It is more efficient to have one company handle the sale and installation, and you will have better recourse later if something goes wrong. Check on extra costs, which can include installation and padding, and the delivery of new and the removal of old carpet.

—Do-it-yourself carpeting is now sold in rolls and in carpet squares or tiles (see p.237, "Do It Yourself").

1. *Construction:* Quality in carpeting is a combination of the kind of fiber and tight construction. The greater the density of the pile or nap (the fibers on the surface of the carpet), the better the resilience and the better the wear. To see how close the strands are to one another, pull the pile aside or open.

The most common methods of carpet manufacture are tufting, needlepunched, or weaving. The pile on carpet can be looped or twisted, shag (long and loose-cut pile), carved or embossed (the pile is cut and shaped to different heights), and velvet (evenly cut pile which gives a smooth appearance). Other novelty methods of construction include needlepoint, hooked and braided.

2. *Fibers:* As a general rule, the best carpeting for a country house is made from synthetic fibers. Most hold color well, clean easily, and are moth-, insect-, and mildew-resistant. Natural fibers, such as wool and cotton, are not as

good. According to Consumer's Research, Inc., wool "is susceptible to moth and beetle damage unless it is treated at the factory (all wool manufactured in this country is supposed to be moth-proof) subject to mildew and weakened by salt." Cotton mats but is inexpensive and can be tossed into a washing machine. However, a wool rug that can be lifted up, aired in the sun and sent to the cleaner may not cause any problem.

Carpet is often made from more than one fiber. A label on all carpeting indicates the fiber content.

Synthetic fibers:

—Acrylic, modacrylic, and nylon have a tendency to pill and fuzz and retain oil stains, but in every other respect—assuming a good-quality construction—particularly resilience and resistance to abrasion and other soiling, they are excellent. Acrylic is considered the fiber that most simulates wool and holds dye the best.

—Polyester is a fiber that holds color very well but has a tendency to crush easily.

—Polypropylene-olefin has a high resistance to stains and fading and low moisture absorbency. Since this fiber is not as resilient and crushes easily, it is usually manufactured in a low pile, tightly woven.

Other natural fibers: Grass, flax, sisal, straw, jute, and raffia are made from natural fibers and these rugs will have a tendency to mildew. However, I have heard more praise than complaints. They are attractive, inexpensive, light in appearance, and easy to maintain; sand and dirt just "disappear" through the cracks. Rugs made from these fibers are apparently not popular with store buyers because, in many areas, they are hard to find.

There are many other kinds of rugs, including rag rugs made from recycled cloth and Indian felt Numdha rugs. They are inexpensive and colorful, but rugs made from recycled rags smell when wet, and felt rugs get very dirty.

3. *Indoor-outdoor carpeting:* Indoor and outdoor carpeting is practical throughout a country home, not just in a

kitchen or outdoors, its principal areas of use. Although all this carpeting can be used indoors, it cannot all be used outdoors. Strictly outdoor carpeting will be so labeled and will have either a synthetic backing (never a sponge or rubber one, which will rot) or no backing at all. Outdoor carpeting, which comes in sheet and tile form, is usually made from acrylic or polypropylene fibers which hold color well and are durable, resistant to stains and water. Outdoor carpeting adds color and a nonslip surface to pool and patio areas that can be swept or hosed down. Some people roll up their outdoor carpeting off-season.

4. *Color and maintenance:* A carpet that conceals dirt best may be textured, patterned, or a tweed in a medium tone. However, there are no hard-and-fast rules, and you must evaluate each carpet as it comes along, taking this and the fiber and construction into account. For example, as I have already pointed out, polypropylene is recommended for kitchens because it is easy to clean and stain-resistant. This does not mean it will conceal dirt. In a dark color every toe of a sandy footstep will show up. Sand and dirt cannot escape into the pile, and so they just lie on top in full view. A shag, on the other hand, absorbs dirt and would appear to be a poor choice of a carpet for a beach house. Some people love shag for just this reason; they never see any footprints or sand or dirt; it all just sinks to the bottom.

5. *Backing and pads:* Backings of jute should be avoided where mildewing is likely to occur and carpet with a synthetic backing used instead.

Pads are placed beneath a carpet and are recommended for longer life and to give a greater feeling of softness underfoot. According to Consumer's Research, pads made in various combinations of hair, foam, and jute show poor resistance to mildew. Therefore, where dampness is a problem, skip the pad.

6. *Seconds and secondhand rugs:* Examine carefully, top and bottom, in a good light.

Rug remnants and mill ends, seconds and irregular carpeting can be an excellent buy for a country house as long as you know what you are getting. Check for imperfections in weave, finish, and color and for a loose backing. If you find some damage, check to make sure you can camouflage or conceal it, like hiding a hole in the rug under the couch.

Secondhand rugs can be examined for the above and in addition for frayed ends, repairs, moths, or insect holes. Smell the rug for rot; look for mildew stains, worn pile and discolorations. (I know someone who recolored a faded rug with permanent magic markers.)

Oriental rugs, either older handmade originals or newer machine-made rugs of Oriental "design," can frequently be found at country shops, auctions, and yard sales. They conceal dirt, are colorful, frequently inexpensive, and they go with just about any decor, modern or traditional. For these reasons, Oriental rugs are perfect for a country house.

RESILIENT FLOORS

—Resilient floor coverings are smooth and hard.

—Most wear well and clean easily. Many are self-polishing, which translated means no waxing.

—If you cannot have real brick, marble, stone, ceramic tile or slate, convincing imitations are made in resilient floorings which are cheaper, softer underfoot, and easier to install.

A floor that is a solid color, smooth, and shiny will show dirt and be harder to maintain than a textured, sculptured, embossed, or speckled surface, which hides irregularities in the floor, dirt, sand and scuff marks. However, if the surface is too deeply sculptured, dirt can become embedded in its cracks, and the floor can be very hard to clean. An old toothbrush helps here. Scratches and sand will show up less on a lighter surface. Medium tones are the best overall dirt disguisers.

Some floor coverings have a felt or felt-and-foam backing which will rot, and these are labeled not to be used where there is moisture, such as on concrete or below grade in the basement. They should probably not be used any place in a damp house.

Before a resilient floor is laid, the floor beneath must be properly prepared. It should be perfectly smooth, and if it is not, a layer of plywood or paper should be put down. Floorboards and bumps below have a way of pushing through a resilient floor, and with wear they will start to show, become unattractive and dirt attracters.

Sheet goods are a better bet than tiles, which have a tendency to shrink and lift up when installed in a house that is damp, subject to leaking, or great changes in temperature as a result of off-season closing. Self-stick do-it-yourself tiles may be more susceptible to popping because the adhesive on the back is often not strong.

1. Sheet Flooring

A major advantage of sheet flooring, available in 6-, 9-, and 12-foot widths, over tiles is that it is continuous with at most one seam. Therefore, it is somewhat sleeker in appearance and a better choice for kitchens and bathrooms where water between cracks can cause tile to loosen. Sheet flooring will not crack or lift off (see above).

Some sheet floors are inexpensive and can be loose laid, not glued down, and then, like a rug, picked up and used again.

Basic types include inlaid vinyl, made by impregnating the design into the vinyl, which is longer lasting than printed vinyl, made by printing the design on top. Printed vinyl or roto-printed vinyl, as it is sometimes called, can be adequate for a house that is used, not abused part time. Linoleum, which wears well, but is limited in color and pattern, cannot be used below grade.

Some sheet flooring has a special cushion backing, making the floor feel softer and warmer underfoot.

2. *Tiles*

Tiles are sold in standard sizes of 9 x 9 inches and 12 x 12 inches. Many are self-adhesive, made for the do-it-yourself market (some of these never need waxing). The principal advantages of tile are its greater design possibilities and easier installation by the nonprofessional. In addition, a damaged tile can be removed and replaced without the purchase of an entire new floor.

If you buy tiles that are sold only in boxes of forty-five, as many are, you may end up paying for more tiles than you need; on the other hand, you should plan on overordering by about 10 percent to allow for waste and replacements.

The most common kinds of tile include vinyl, which is the most expensive but also the most resilient, is the least likely to crack, and is manufactured in the most sophisticated patterns; vinyl asbestos, which is a good substitute for vinyl and less expensive; and asphalt, also low-cost but brittle—it absorbs grease, needs waxing, and is not recommended for a country home.

Feature strips are narrow bands of resilient floor material used in combination with tiles to create special designs.

Building Materials

You may be lucky enough to have or inherit a house with beautiful hard-surface floors of slate, ceramic tile, flagstone, terrazzo, or brick, easy to clean, with zero maintenance. These floors are not only hardy (they'll last longer than you will), but hard underfoot, and unless the floor below is heated, they can feel icy cold.

—Terrazzo is made of small chips of marble or other rock and cement; it is a surface that is poured on and must be sealed.

—Glazed ceramic tile is available in assorted shapes, including the classic hexagon, and in many sizes. Tiles should specify that they are floor, not wall, tiles. A mat finish will be less slippery than a shiny one. While the tiles themselves require practically no attention, the grout between the tiles can become dirty. A medium- to dark-colored grout will not show the dirt; a white grout can be cleaned with a cotton swab and bleach.

—Slate, flagstone, brick and quarry tile are also available in many colors and shapes. They can be left as is or stained. I know someone who uses shoe polish paste wax on brick with great success. All are porous and must be properly sealed.

WOOD

There is nothing richer than the color and texture of a wood floor, the most common and often the easiest kind of floor to maintain. The appearance of the floor is a combination of the kind of wood, the way it is laid, and the way it is finished. A new wood floor may be installed in parquet pattern or planks of all the same or random widths. Some new wood floors have wood pegs that simulate dowels found in older floors. A wood floor may be left *au naturel* and simply sealed or stained and sealed. A protective finish is normally recommended, either of wax, which then requires periodic rewaxing, or of varnish, such as polyurethane, which requires nothing more than an occasional mop. A plastic varnish will scratch and eventually wear off. When it does, the whole floor must be refinished. But this could take years.

Don't give up on a wood floor that is in poor condition. Try to renew it with a good waxing (the wax has a cleaning agent in it), or you can go all the way and have it scraped down and refinished. See p.238, for do-it-yourself instructions.

Properly sealed wood floors are used today all over the house, including the bathroom and kitchen.

For lowest maintenance, use a polyurethane finish on a floor that is medium to light in color. Dark-colored floors, though elegant, seem to show every speck of dirt. Wood

Vinyl tile in a checkerboard pattern. The radiator becomes part of the decor when it is painted the color of tile and covered with a shelf.

floors with painted finishes are very popular in country homes as a colorful, inexpensive, and quick cover-up. It is easier for a do-it-yourselfer to paint a floor than to scrape, stain, and finish one, and although colored stains are available for floors, the choice and intensity of color are much greater with paint. On the minus side, paint, which lies on top of the floor surface (as opposed to stain, which is rubbed into the floor), will chip and usually needs an annual touch-up. A white painted floor will also yellow and need refreshening with a new coat of paint. A strong color may rub off slightly when mopping, so use separate mops for colored and white floors.

Continuous Seamless Flooring or Poured-On Floors

In a class by itself this product is a mixed breed. It resembles paint, is applied like terrazzo. Poured on, it looks like sheet vinyl without any seams when dry. A plastic embedded with tiny chips, it can be installed by amateur or professional.

Curtains of striped canvas that match seat cushions can be closed
for privacy and protection from rain.

CHAPTER SEVEN

OUTSIDE AREAS

No matter how comfortable your country home may be, the most enjoyable and relaxing part of life there will generally be the time you spend outdoors. Indeed, in warm weather, most activities will take place there, and the hours spent in the house will be remembered merely as a measure of the summer's rainfall.

Most city dwellers tend to be indoors-oriented on matters of design and give little thought to the planning and decoration of the outdoor areas. There must be adequate provision for playing, lounging, sunbathing, cooking, dining, entertaining, and perhaps even sleeping or at least napping. There must be facilities for hiding unsightly garbage cans and garden equipment so that they will be accessible but not too visible. There must be protection against the sun, insects, and the curious eyes of neighbors, and to be truly successful, the design and color of the outdoor areas, including flowers, fences, lighting, furniture, floor and wall coverings, must echo the decoration of the house of which they are an extension.

Outdoor Rooms

While a hammock under a tree or an umbrella table may fully satisfy the needs of one family, more may be required by another, anything from a privacy fence to a screened-in porch. In designing an outdoor enclosure, consider how much sun, air, and view to let in, as well as how much heat, wind, rain, and how many insects and neighbors to keep out. A house may have built-in protection in the form of deep roof overhangs, natural shrubbery, and a good orientation to winds and sun. All that may be necessary is to set two lounge chairs on the grass and start sunning.

The relation of the house to the sun can determine whether you will have shade or sun, ideally both at different hours, when and where. The side that faces east will get morning sun, which is cooler, the west side will get hot afternoon sun, and the southern exposure will get a little of both. Knowing this, you will not build a sun deck on the north side, which gets virtually no sun at all. An outdoor structure can be located outside any room in the house. For example, another place to enjoy nature and a private retreat away from the rest of the household would be created by building a simple deck off the master bedroom.

Different kinds of enclosures that are part of a house include patios, porches, terraces, decks, lanais, and atria. Independent structures are gazebos (an open garden house usually with seating), playhouses, greenhouses, utility houses, pool or boathouses, tree houses, and these, in turn, may have their own patios, decks, etc.

An overhead roof on a structure will shield the sun, cut down on heat, and protect against the rain. Side walls on a structure (as well as certain kinds of fences and hedges), depending on their degree of solidity or transparency, will protect against nosy neighbors, wind, and sun.

The amount of enclosure can be flexible. An awning can sometimes be moved back and forth, and bamboo blinds can go up and down; an insulated porch can have screens in the summer and glass windows in the winter for year-round pleasure.

1. Overhead: The Roof

Analyze how much overhead protection is desirable and whether it should be permanent, removable, adjustable, transparent, or opaque. Different kinds include:

Open areas: *Above*, a deck with water bed for sunbathing and low chairs for lounging. *Below*, flagstone patio shaded by walls of house and tree.

Enclosed outdoor rooms: *Above*, an unheated but enclosed porch with a variety of furniture, including a park bench and director's chair, made to conform with white paint. *Below*, although geranium trees, a sisal rug painted green, and trellis around windows and door impart an outdoor feeling, this summer room is very much an indoor room, fully insulated and heated. *Opposite*, sitting room completely enclosed in glass and heated. Beams in roof radiate from a center glass cupola; overhangs block sun.

Partially protected outdoor areas: *Above*, overhead protection on a balcony overlooking Palm Beach and the ocean (furniture is fiberglass with vinylized cushions, floors are ceramic tile). *Below*, an open porch in Lake Placid. *Opposite, top*, tent and umbrella table block the hot Florida sun. *Below*, a poolside gazebo with fencing found in a cemetery.

—An extension of the roof of the house.

—An open lattice roof made of wood strips (lath) that are spaced apart and supported by beams and crosspieces, like an overhead trellis. The closer the pieces of lathing, the heavier the vines growing over it, the more protection from the rays of the sun and the wind. No protection against rain but cooler than a solid cover because it allows for air circulation.

—A solid wood framed roof with fiber glass, plastic, or aluminum panels, solid or (with the exception of aluminum) translucent or transparent, depending on how much light you want to let in. Rainproof.

—An awning made of canvas that is as lightproof as possible and waterproof, stretched over and attached to a metal frame. May be adjustable.

2. Underfoot: Floors

The surface of outdoor areas should be easy to maintain, not slippery, coordinated with the design and floor of the house, if not actually a continuation of it, and weather-resistant, if exposed. Determine how much hard flooring, paths, driveways, in addition to patios and enclosed areas, you want in relation to the amount of sand or grass. While it may not be as lush as grass, you don't have to mow cement. Inquire locally about problems of cracking and buckling owing to changes in temperature and establish whether the floor material will retain heat and be too hot to walk on in bare feet. Look into outdoor floors that can be a do-it-yourself project.

Any surface that is planned should be large enough so that furniture will not dangle half off and half on.

Kinds of outdoor floor materials include:

—Temporary: ground covers such as gravel, wood chips, and crushed rocks.

—Semipermanent: indoor-outdoor carpeting; make sure it is so labeled. (See p.167.)

Underfoot: brick, flagstone slabs, stones, grass, and asphalt.

—Permanent: flagstone, slate, concrete and concrete blocks, stone, brick, ceramic tile, and wood.

Look around your area, particularly the grounds of a house that is being demolished, for secondhand bricks, flagstone, stone, and slate with a beautiful patina.

A word on wood: Strips for wood decks should be far enough apart to allow for drainage. A wood preservative increases the life of the wood and protects it from damage by moisture and insects. Stain and paint may be esthetically pleasing, but they must be renewed. Blocks or rounds of wood tend to split in the cold and to warp in the heat. Woods commonly used for outdoor floors include fir, cedar, redwood, pine, and cypress. Lumber that is directly next to the soil should be heartwood, the center core of the log, because it is more resistant to decay than sapwood.

3. On the Side: Fences, Walls, and Screens

Fences, walls, and screens can hide an ugly view of garbage cans or other houses, keep children off the road or out of the pool, block or baffle wind, and give privacy and shade (depending on their degree of transparency). If your objective is to shield your home from view, a solid wall will be your choice, and can be constructed from concrete, brick, wood, metal or canvas stretched on a frame. On the other hand, if your purpose is simply to keep the kids out of trouble, an open wall, which will not block light, air, or view, may be preferable and can be constructed from any building material spaced apart. A wall of translucent plastic or glass will permit the light in, while one of transparent plastic or glass will permit both light and an unimpeded view. Some walls are adjustable, such as folding screens with casters on the bottom (for easy opening and closing).

Esthetics are another consideration. An unusual wall can be a decorative asset but it should relate in color, material and design to the house. For example, a picket fence would look silly around a modern structure and a wall of decora-

Exterior walls: *Above (left)*, folding louvered panels and *(right)*, cement block arranged in a honeycomb pattern. *Below*, canvas stretched on wood framing.

tive concrete block absurd around a log cabin. After considering the various styles available, custom made or stock, high or low, plain or fancy, and deciding on your needs, be sure to check local building codes on height and location of fences or walls. And if what you want is not permitted, hedges may be a suitable alternative.

Casual and Outdoor Furniture

With the same care you used to plan interior spaces, decide what you need and how you want to arrange it. Measure your space and consider the size and kind of furnishings you want to go there; you may be surprised to find out how much room bulky outdoor furniture can take up. On the other hand, use the minimum amount of furniture necessary. While only two chairs in a room indoors might look strange, the same two chairs outdoors set out on a wide expanse of lawn would not. For typical sizes of furniture, see p. 70.

What Kind and Where

—For sunning and sitting: chaise longue, armchair and ottoman, couch, chairs.

—For eating: chairs and tables, barbecue.

—For drinking: bar for storage and for serving drinks.

—For entertainment: storage for games, outdoor equipment, music.

Planters and assorted extra tables to hold drinks, ashtrays, telephone, lamps. Enough room left to move around.

Casual or "outdoor" furniture should be:

1. *Portable:* Foldable or stackable, it should be lightweight or on wheels so it can be moved into or out of the sun, wherever needed, and easily stored out of season (if it cannot be moved, cover it with plastic).

Tables and chairs that fold up and disappear are convenient. A small family may need only a small table for

Above, rattan hanging chairs, varnished for outdoor use and suspended from a wooden frame. *Below*, a German *Strandkorb* has adjustable back and awning, footrests that pull out, even a place to lock up belongings.

outdoor eating or none at all, but it might be handy to have a large dining table and chairs that could be pulled out for company, such as inexpensive folding aluminum tables, or large table tops that go over and enlarge a table, or small snack tables and folding chairs. Or:

2. *Built-in:* Neat in appearance and easy to maintain, built-ins take up less room and can be an integral part of the design of a house. The most common are tables and benches, but I have also seen wood chaises built into a deck. The top of a retaining wall, a box built around the base of a tree, several large rocks or a tree stump could qualify as built-in furniture.

3. *Comfortable:* Soft and deep, a chaise or armchair should make you relax. Test it out before buying because some outdoor furniture feels hard and might be comfortable enough for sitting up but not for reclining.

4. *Sturdy:* All outdoor furniture should be subject to the same scrutiny as indoor furniture (see p. 104), tested for sturdiness of construction and examined for quality of workmanship.

5. *Easily maintained:* Durable, stain- and weather-resistant (both frame and covering), depending on how exposed it will be to the elements, and easy to clean. Most furniture with a paint finish will chip and will need an annual spruce-up, with exterior paint if it is used outdoors. A new coat of color can be added to fabric and vinyl with Fabspray (see p.230,"Do It Yourself").

The fewer exposed metal parts, the better because most rust. If rusting does occur, loosen it by rubbing with steel wool, wire brush, or sandpaper and a rust remover or lemon juice. Cover a rusty painted surface with metal primer, and then repaint. Incidentally, dark-colored metal furniture will not show rust as easily as light-colored. A protective film should come between the weather and metal, such as a water-repellent finish of paint, lacquer, wax, or clear silicone. Glass wax is an excellent covering for chrome.

Rust and other stains on fabric are best treated at the dry

cleaner's. At home, remove rust spots by moistening the stain with lemon juice and salt; then dry in the sun.

MATERIALS FOR THE OUTDOORS

The term "outdoor furniture" is misleading; much of the furniture that is so loosely labeled cannot withstand the rigors of the outdoors. It should be called casual or summer furniture. On the other hand, the word "outdoor" can apply to an area that is shielded from the elements. When choosing furniture, keep in mind where it is to be used and draw a distinction between furniture that will be kept permanently out in the open completely exposed to the weather and furniture that will be partially protected under a lanai or fully protected in an insulated enclosed porch. In the following section I use the word "outdoor" literally, as exposed to wind, rain, and storm.

—Redwood is completely weather-resistant, excellent outdoors, especially at the beach. However, this furniture is bulky, and the chairs and chaises are uncomfortable in the absence of cushions. If the cushions aren't waterproof or water-repellent (see p. 193) and are left out in the rain by mistake, it can take your whole vacation for them to dry out. Redwood usually needs a refreshening each season with redwood stain and sealer. By the way, redwood is not red— it is white.

—Director's chairs are made of canvas and wood and are excellent outdoors. A painted finish can be renewed with paint—a can of spray enamel is handiest—and the canvas can be either renewed with Fabspray, painted with acrylic paint, or replaced inexpensively. Personalize these with *permanent* magic markers.

—Rattan, wicker, and other natural woven fibers should not be used outdoors unless coated with varnish (and then with some caution) and in semiprotected areas or indoor areas of country homes. Loose strands can be reglued, and chipped or soiled surfaces of painted rattan or wicker repainted.

Almost free—and easy to make—outdoor tables: *Opposite, top*, a concrete slab on cement blocks; *center*, on two clay chimney flues, a piece of marble; *bottom*: a slate slab barrel; *on this page*, a piece of driftwood and a garden gate.

—Molded plastic is very weather-resistant and fine out-doors, but it scratches easily, and cushionless plastic chairs or chaise longues can be hard and uncomfortable. Some plastic furniture floats and is fun to use in a swimming pool. Available in many qualities from cheap to expensive, it is easily cleaned with soap and water (never with an abrasive) and can be Simonized for protection against scratching. For plastic table tops, see below.

—Inflatable plastic is also very weather-resistant if it lasts that long. Even the best quality may leak, and all of it punctures easily. Punctures can be repaired with a tape made for this purpose. There are many satisfied owners of plastic inflated water beds which can be used out on a deck for sunning.

—Aluminum is rust-resistant. It is the most common and versatile metal used in the manufacture of both the cheapest and most expensive outdoor furniture. Tubular aluminum furniture with plastic webbing will pit at the beach, and it is so lightweight it might blow away in a strong wind. But because of its price, the lowest of all outdoor furniture, it is a good bet and can easily be replaced, or restored with new webbing and a scrubbing with steel wool and detergent. More costly varieties of aluminum are welded, wrought, extruded, and mixed with other alloys. They usually have a protective finish which makes them completely weather-resistant.

—Steel with a baked enamel finish will eventually chip and rust but is adequate in outdoor situations away from the beach.

—Wrought iron rusts and should not be used outdoors unless it is covered with a good-quality outdoor paint.

Table top materials include:

—Glass may be frosted or clear (shows fingermarks and people's legs beneath the table). Tempered glass is heat-resistant and, if it breaks, will shatter into many small pieces instead of breaking into a few and potentially more dangerous large ones.

—Fiber glass and acrylic are break-resistant and heat-resistant, but they may scratch, and certain chemicals may stain them.

—Metal: See above.

Umbrellas come in vinyl or canvas. The vinyl is easy to clean and will last a long time, although it may eventually crack. Umbrellas should be stored in a dry, moderate temperature and anchored beneath tables with either a 50- or 100-pound weight, depending on the wind. Old ratty-looking fringe should be removed and new fringe sewn on, or attached with a water-resistant glue.

Seat coverings, cushions, and fabric are almost never waterproof, so if in doubt assume that they are not. To be truly "waterproof," a cushion cannot have perforations—*i.e.*, no stitching. Instead the cushion must be heat-sealed. To be "water-repellent," a cushion should be filled with polyester or urethane foam, which dries faster and does not mildew, and covered with vinyl, canvas with a vinyl coating, or plastic. Unfortunately, the labeling I have seen indicates only the kind of stuffing, not the covering material, and does not tell the customer whether or not the cushion is water-repellent or waterproof. Fabric that is used on outdoor furniture should be mildew-resistant, at least water-repellent and colorfast, easy to clean and resistant to soil. Acrylic canvas and vinyl (although it "sticks") are good choices here. Cotton can be finished with a plastic coating to make it waterproof or Zepel and Scotchgard to make it water- and stain-resistant.

If the fabric cannot be wiped clean, then removable washable cushion covers should be used. Cushions that are a standard size and style can be easily replaced when necessary.

To avoid the on-again off-again problem of cushions, select outdoor furniture that has plastic webbing or Dacron mesh seats or backs and therefore requires no cushion and no attention other than an occasional wipe-off with soap and water.

Unusual planters: *Clockwise from top left*, the inside of a discarded washing machine; a lavabo; a giant can; a basket.

Lawn Lighting and Accessories

LIGHTING

Outdoor lighting can be practical for safety and protection at night to illuminate paths and steps and the front door, ornamental, or both at once. Strong light such as spotlights can light up a garden, trees and driveway, and softer lights such as low lights near the ground can light up a path or patio. For parties, torches, candles, and strings of colored lights set a mood while illuminating. Lights can be attached to a house, a tree, fence, or dock or stuck in the ground.

Although there are some do-it-yourself low-voltage systems, generally the installation of outdoor wiring should be left to experts. Wires, electric boxes, light fixtures, and switches must be waterproof. Wires can be strung along on the ground and wound through trees, but it is best if they are buried under the ground. Provision for outdoor lighting should be made when a house is built.

Lighting a lawn is a specialty. Even a good electrician may not know how to install it properly for maximum effect. Short of calling in a lighting expert or landscape architect, you should experiment yourself before permanently installing light fixtures. The source of light should always be concealed; it should not shine into your face. The overall appearance should be soft and subtle and not look like a lit-up baseball field. Try colored lights. Yellow ones are antibug; others cast unusual colors on an area.

PLANTERS

While a discussion of landscaping is beyond the scope of this book, the use of plants and planters on decks and patios certainly is not, and it is an important part of decorating a country home.

Planters and plants can carry out the decorating theme

Above, for the house, a chimney dec
oration. *Left,* for the birds, a feede
from a cooking pan placed on a pos
Opposite, special swimming pool dec
orations: A painted poolside and (*be
low*) a waterfall at the foot of
free-form pool.

Garden sculpture: *Clockwise, from top*, ceramic pig; statuesque driftwood; sand-casted shapes of the seashore. *Opposite*, a modern sculpture of sand-blasted steel.

and add softness and color. Large shrubs and small trees can be practical, blocking out wind and a view of the house next door while controlling the flow of traffic in and around the patio. Just about anything can be used for a planter as long as it sits on the ground, hangs from wall or roof, and has proper drainage, either a hole or a layer of broken clay at the bottom. Commercially made planters are available in wood, fiber glass, concrete, stone, or metal. Since these can be expensive, it might be a good idea to think of things around the house that would be good substitutes, such as boxes, buckets, bushel baskets, tubs, flue liners, the liner from a discarded washing machine. Planters I have used include an old bathtub, a coal grate, and a lavabo. Save nicely shaped liquor, salad dressing, or soda bottles for cut flowers.

Extra advice: There is nothing more pathetic than an empty window box in winter; to restore it to usefulness, fill it with many branches of evergreen.

OTHER DECORATING ACCESSORIES

Sculpture and statuary, fountains and pools can be used effectively in an outdoor area so long as they are in scale, not too large and overpowering or too small and insignificant, and in character with the house. A marble statue might be fine in a formal garden but would look ridiculous at a beach house, where a do-it-yourself driftwood piece would be more appropriate.

CHAPTER EIGHT

DECORATING MYTHS OF SEA AND SKI HOUSES

The house shown on the jacket of this book is at the beach, but if the view outside didn't give it away, you might just as easily place it at a ski resort. With few exceptions, climate or area have less and less effect on the design of a country home, and an A frame is just as likely to be found up north as down south, at the beach as on a mountaintop. Except for regional styles, it follows that the differences in interior design owing to area are few. The fact that a country home may be owner-occupied or rented out year-round under varied weather conditions and not used only for summer or ski weekends makes generalizations about decor that much more difficult. Following are the few distinctions that might be made:

—A ski house is largely inner-directed. Therefore, it is possibly more important to have a large indoor play area than exterior patios and porches. But most ski houses have or should have decks for use in or out of the ski season.

—While every home needs storage space and extra sleeping quarters, the quota for a ski house filled with bulky clothing and equipment and a guest for every child may be higher. Equipment should be stored in a mud room that not only has room for ski racks and a place to hang clothes but, to avoid a mess in the house, is large enough for everybody to move around or sit down in to change clothing. Guests can be stored in bunk rooms.

—Bedrooms in all country places can be compact, and

201

Fireplaces at the beach: *Top*, *left*, modern metal, prefabricated, free-standing, and compact silhouetted against window, it looks like sculpture. *Top right*, fieldstone fireplace focal point of a cozy conversation pit. The coffee table base was inspired by the chandelier and made by the builder. *Below*, a stucco fireplace with illuminated niches for display.

Three kinds of brickwork: *Above*, *left*, modern-style fireplace, brick laid in a header bond (the short way but flat); *at right*, Louis-XV-style fireplace, brick laid in a herringbone pattern. *Below*, Colonial-style fireplace, brick laid in a stretcher bond.

Lighting: *Opposite, top left*, steering wheel and lantern. *Top right*, chandeliers made from graters. *Bottom left*, funny floor light made from odds and ends. *Bottom right*, floor-to-ceiling paper lamp. *On this page, clockwise from top left*, plants hanging from candlelit chandelier; inverted potato chip can with fringe and star appliqué glued on; brandy-keg lamp base; a chandelier made from tennis ball cans.

Bars: *Opposite*, *top*, a dry sink; a cabinet sink. *Below*, an armoire fitted with refrigerator; a wooden icebox. *On this page*, *top*, a peanut vendor's wagon. *Below*, a Belgian stove with glass shelves above it.

HOT
ROASTED

Bar closets: *Top*, *left*: arched niche fitted with cabinet, liquor racks, and chandelier could be created from a closet. *Right*, a closet converted to a bar by adding shelves, decorating it with wallpaper and mirror. *Bottom*, in a Palm Beach foyer a bronze plexiglass panel, between vertical bands of light, opens to reveal a bar.

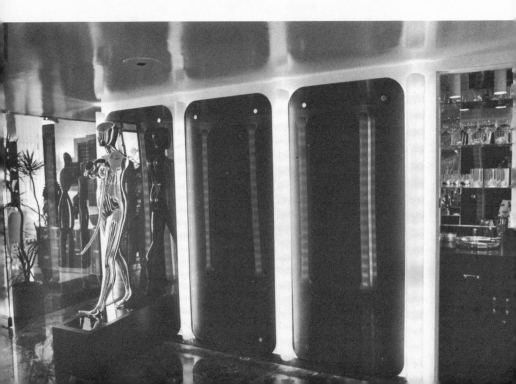

most people agree that in ski houses particularly, closet space is more important than floor space.

—While glowing coals and crackling flames are an integral part of a ski vacation, a fireplace is just as likely to be the focal point of a beach house and to be equally useful. Today a home with a fireplace is no longer a luxury. All kinds of prefabricated fireplaces are available from modern to traditional. Frequently low in cost and easy to install—with no special structural requirements—some styles may be built in, others are free standing; some can be attached to an existing flue, others are equipped with their own flue.

—Salt air corrodes, so care should be taken in the selection and maintenance of metal furniture and accessories in a beach house.

—The climate might affect the choice of materials that look and feel either cool or warm. In a ski house carpeting and woolly textured fabrics are "cozier," while ceramic tile and cotton canvas are probably better suited to warmer weather.

Mildew and fading can occur anywhere. A beach house that is well ventilated may not be as damp as a poorly ventilated house in a dry area; the glare of the sun is strong whether it is reflected off snow or sand. Bright or neutral color schemes should be chosen according to preference and practical considerations not location.

CHAPTER NINE

THE UNOCCUPIED HOUSE

The new homeowner will soon discover that the period when his country home is subject to the greatest abuse is not when the children are running in and out, but when the house is unoccupied. It is then that the house is prey to vandals and vulnerable to the perils of fire, broken pipes, and a flooded basement. For the unwary owner, the off-season may be the expensive season.

The precautions required when the house is unoccupied will depend on a variety of factors: climate, location, length of time the house will be unoccupied and the value of the contents of the house. There are several things you can do to protect an empty house:

—Notify neighbors and the police that you are leaving and tell them to call you if they see any suspicious activity. A very neighborly neighbor may agree to look over and into the house from time to time.

—Give a neighbor a key or hide one on the premises so that, when necessary, someone can get into the house on your instruction.

—Install an alarm system. Some people just buy the stickers, not the system. A gadget that turns a light on at night just the way you would if you were home might be a wise and inexpensive investment.

—Arrange for the house to be occupied by someone else when you are not there. Rent it out or give it to a "house sitter" to live in free, in exchange for taking care of and doing odd jobs around the house (sometimes this is not worth the risks involved). Lend it to friends. Always leave another occupant with a list of local service people and instructions on how to work appliances so you won't be awakened in the middle of the night and asked how to fix the furnace.

One of the great advantages of homes that are part of resort developments or condominiums attached to a hotel is that they are maintained and patrolled by a permanent staff.

CLOSING UP

All the following remarks may not apply to houses that are unoccupied for short periods of time, several days between weekends, but most apply to those permanently closed for an extended period of time or for several months. There will be fewer problems closing a winter house, such as a ski house, for the summer, than vice versa. Short of just locking the door and walking out, here's a checklist of some things to keep you busy closing up:

—Store outdoor furniture.

—Pack clothing and equipment to be taken with you.

—Have house cleaned; in some areas there is a service that performs this chore.

—Send rugs, slip covers, etc. to the local cleaner.

—Empty refrigerator and freezer. If you are going to turn the electricity off, leave refrigerator doors open. If you plan to be back soon, leave food in the freezer. A good way to tell whether food has defrosted is to put an ice cube in a dish in the freezer; if it has melted and lost its form, then you know the freezer has gone off.

—Throw out boxes of grain and cereals. Don't leave bottles of liquids in an unheated area because they may freeze and burst.

—To avoid mildew from moisture in a house without heat, put mothballs under and on top of mattresses and in closets, and hang large Endew bags all over. Leave clothes hanging loose in closets, not in bags, and if electricity is to be kept on, install an electric dehumidifier to cut down on closet dampness.

—Cover beds and unholstered furniture with plastic, for special protection from dust and leaks.

—To protect against the invasion of animals, close the damper of the fireplace and cover the top of the chimney with wire mesh. Similarly cover stovepipes and make sure all other openings, such as vents in a crawl space, are screened if they are left open.

—If the threat of animals coming in and chewing up all your bedding is a real one, remove it and store in metal-lined containers, or if there are open beams in the ceiling, hang it from them.

—Pull down shades or blinds.

—If it is necessary, put up storm windows or board windows.

—Stop local deliveries—newspaper, milk—and stop or reduce garbage pickup. If the heat is turned off, stop fuel deliveries.

—Disconnect the telephone.

—If a house in a cold area will be closed (*i.e.*, the heat and electricity turned off), drain all pipes to avoid freezing and bursting. A local plumber can do this for you.

—Turn off the gas; turn off electricity by disconnecting the main switch. To guard against some one else turning it off by mistake or on purpose, you may want to consider locking the central switch that is on the exterior of a house.

—If the heat is to be kept on, and this can be expensive, turn it down to around 60 degrees.

—Water plants in absentia by using a $2 device sold for this purpose, or you can water plants before leaving and then cover them with a plastic bag.

—Hire a house watcher or protection agency. In fancier circles and in olden days known as caretakers, they do basically the same thing, but cost far less. A local person, the gardener or the baby-sitter, may want to earn extra income this way. Local tradespeople or classified listings will have names of people and businesses who provide this service.

This is what a house watcher should do:

If the house is closed up with all utilities shut off, then the job is fairly simple; look around outside for damage owing to wear, vandals, or acts of God, then check inside to make sure there hasn't been any foul play. Double check that doors and windows are locked.

If the house is semi-open—that is, the electricity has been left on but turned low—do all the above and, in addition, check that electricity and heat haven't gone off, causing freezing pipes. Check the basement for floods. If the principal fear is frozen pipes, then the house may be "watched" only when the temperature goes below freezing.

A house watcher can also arrange to have things repaired or to repair them himself; to receive packages; to water plants; to rake leaves; shovel snow; and to perform various other chores that continue regardless of whether the owner is there.

OPENING UP

This should be a simple matter of plugging in, turning on, and airing out. If air is damp, turn up the heat, open the windows and put musty-smelling furnishings, such as mattresses, out to sun. If you are lucky, that will be all. However, when a house hasn't been used for a long time, the list of things to do can really pile up, for example:

ONE COUNTRY HOMEOWNER'S
TO-DO LIST THIS WEEK

1. Call plumber to fix leak. Fix pump. Find out why it burst and flooded cellar.

2. Call washing machine repairman. Washing machine has died (of loneliness? Repairman says it will cost only $80 and take only two months to get a new part, and then he

can't be sure it will work. Says it is an old machine, three years old, and should be replaced).

3. Call tree service. Weeping willows have something to cry about.

4. Call refrigerator repairman. Refrigerator making strange noises. (He comes, clips the same little rubber tube at the bottom that he cuts each time, no matter what's wrong, $27.50.)

5. Call kitchen planning service. Need a dishwasher; may have to redo whole kitchen and increase wiring service to fit one in; therefore, get name of electrician.

6. Call stove repairman. Coils in oven heating unit broken ($35 plus labor, two visits, and a long wait for the part; oh, well, if I don't cook, I won't have dirty dishes, so I won't need a dishwasher).

7. Buy paint and calking, for painter to paint dock and deck, calk around windows and doors. (Can't do it myself, too busy on the telephone.)

8. Call garbage pickup. They haven't picked up garbage from last summer!

9. Call heating man. Come quickly; soot all over the cellar going through ducts to house; pipe connecting to heater has burst.

10. Make a set of duplicate keys, so that all these people can get into the house while I am away at a hotel.

This girl's camp office was, appropriately, decorated by the campers: The rug was made from carpet remnants and samples, the curtain from felt squares sewed together and tied with yarn to the rod; the walls were covered with self-adhesive plastic; the stool was recovered and the pillow embroidered.

CHAPTER TEN

DO-IT-YOURSELF SHORTCUTS

Buying a country home to putter around in and fix up may be one person's idea of heaven, but just as many other homeowners do it themselves simply as a matter of necessity.

This chapter is dedicated to those who would prefer to be out fishing than home refinishing furniture and describes how to renovate and decorate furniture, floors, windows, and walls with a minimum expenditure of time and effort. Here are the ground rules:

—Buy materials that are made for the do-it-yourself market or intrinsically easy to use. These are plentiful. A well-stocked hardware, paint, or home-building center is the best source of information on what is available.

—Get as many facts as possible from store personnel on how to use a product and read the manufacturer's instructions and labels, carefully *before beginning*, not after, to find out what went wrong.

—Make sure all tools and materials are on hand in adequate supply to complete the job. Check "kits" for completeness. Out in the country, supplies are not as readily available, and stores may close for the weekend.

—Be honest about your talent and time; do not be overambitious. Start small. If you have never painted or papered a room, begin with a bathroom, not a ballroom.

—Test before beginning. For example, try a furniture finish out in an inconspicuous spot.

—Find friends and neighbors to help. Do not rely too

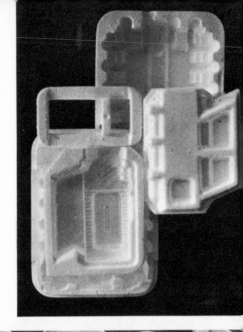

Art from free materials:
Clockwise, *from top left*,
sponges painted different colors; styrofoam packing pieces;
wood scraps, the builder's leftovers; a bird of painted rocks;
driftwood.

heavily on children. Always enthusiastic about a project at first and often remarkably handy, they have a limited attention span, especially on sunny summer days.

—Try to allocate some area in the house as a work area. A basement is ideal, but even a corner of a garage or a small closet will do.

—Assemble a basic box of tools. Include screwdrivers (regular and Phillips), wrench, chisel, putty knife, hammer, saw, pliers, high-compression stapler, scissors, drill and clamps, measuring tools (metal tape, yardstick, folding wood rule), adhesives (white glue, contact cement, spray adhesive, epoxy glue, Duco cement, Scotch, masking and double-faced tape), fine and coarse sandpaper, fine steel wool, single-edge razor blades, paint brushes and rollers of assorted sizes, solvents (benzene, denatured alcohol, turpentine). Assorted tacks, nails, and screws, bolts and plugs, including common nails (big head) and finishing nails or brads (small head), plaster or masonry nails, picture hangers, toggle or molly bolts (for inserting screws into a sheetrock wall), or plugs (for inserting screws into masonry walls).

A *tall* ladder is essential if you plan to do any wallpapering.

This list of basics is only the beginning and the committed do-it-yourselfer will want to add many other things, including electric saw and drill, professional spray paint machine or sewing machine. In some areas it may be possible to rent power hand tools.

—Buy or borrow books (see bibliography) for more specific information on how to do the projects suggested in the next sections.

How Much Material?

When estimating amounts, take care not to confuse inches with feet and yards. And be generous. It is better to have leftovers than not enough.

WALLS

The following formulas are based on covering all the walls in a room and should be adapted for fewer than four walls.

To calculate the number of square feet of wall to be covered in the entire room, multiply the perimeter, the number of linear feet going all around the room, by the height of the room in feet. (The ceiling area will be the width times the length.) To calculate the number of square feet of one wall multiply the width by the height of that wall.

Paint

The average gallon of paint covers roughly 350 to 400 square feet. The label on the can may indicate the covering power of that particular paint. Increase the amount if the ceiling, closets, built-ins, radiators, etc. are to be painted, if more than one coat will be necessary, and if the paint is thick or the wall very porous.

Wallpaper

Wallpaper is made in single, double, or triple rolls. Each single roll of wallpaper has 36 square feet of material, about 30 square feet of it usable, allowing for waste and matching of patterns. Divide the number of square feet to be covered by 30 to find out how many rolls you need. Then deduct one single roll for every two openings or two single rolls for every three openings: windows, doors, and fireplaces. Leftover wallpaper can be used for patching and to cover or trim furniture and accessories such as lamps and picture frames.

Paneling

Using a standard-size panel 4 x 8 feet and assuming a

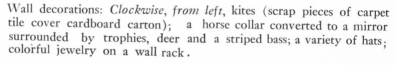

Wall decorations: *Clockwise, from left,* kites (scrap pieces of carpet tile cover cardboard carton); a horse collar converted to a mirror surrounded by trophies, deer and a striped bass; a variety of hats; colorful jewelry on a wall rack.

room height of no more than 8 feet, divide the perimeter of the room by 4. Round out to the next highest number. Deduct one-half panel each for openings—door, windows, fireplace.

Fabric

Divide the width of the fabric in inches into the perimeter, translated into inches. Round out to the next highest number. This figure is the number of panels of fabric necessary. The length of each panel will be the height of the room plus the length of the repeat if the fabric has a pattern to be matched plus 3 inches for trimming. Translate into yards. Multiply the number of yards in each panel by the number of panels necessary to get total yardage required.

FLOORS

To calculate the number of square feet of floor, multiply the length of the room by the width, in feet. This figure will also be the number of 12- x 12-inch tiles. If tiles are 9 x 9 inches, use this formula: $\dfrac{L \times W \times 16}{9}$ (length and width calculated in feet)

If floor material is sold by the square yard, divide by 9.

UPHOLSTERY AND SLIP COVERS

Both the pattern and width of fabric and the style of furniture affect yardage requirements. The following figures are minimums based on plain, patternless fabric 54 inches wide. Check them against your own calculations by measuring the furniture or the covering that has been removed from it. Slip covers require slightly more yardage.

Club chair: 6½ yards tight back; 7½ yards loose pillow back.

Wing chair: 6½ yards.

Easy but elegant reupholstery: A beautiful crochet throw, draped over a chaise lounge.

Ottoman: 3 yards with semi-attached cushion; 2 yards with no cushion.

Sofa: 15 yards for 7-foot sofa with tight back and three seat cushions and skirt; 17–18 yards for 7-foot sofa with loose pillow back cushions and three seat cushions and skirt.

Make back and arm covers from excess fabric.

CURTAINS

Measure the width of the rod or the area to be covered in inches, and add on 12 inches for overlap and returns. For double full curtains multiply by two, and for triple full curtains multiply by three. Divide by the number of inches in the width of the fabric, and round off to the next highest number. This is the number of panels of fabric necessary. Measure the length desired, and add 8 inches for heading and hems and, if patterned, the length of one design repeat. Multiply the length by the number of panels; then translate inches into yards.

Repairing, Renewing, and Refinishing Furniture

The following is basic information on how to repair, renew, or refinish old castoffs, pieces inherited with a house or from family or friends.

Place furniture you are fixing up on a table or a carton that is off the floor within easy reach.

Fill in holes and dents with wood filler. Remove old glue by scraping off, and reglue with white glue where necessary. Hold tight with a clamp or string pulled taut.

Do not assume that every dingy-looking piece of wood furniture needs a complete refinish. Refinishing can reduce the value of an antique, and a good piece should be professionally restored. First, try cleaning. Wipe off old wax with turpentine; rub white spots with 000 grade steel wool and lemon oil. Then wipe with a damp cloth and a mild soap. Fill in scratches with Old English Scratch Cover, eyebrow

Renewing without refinishing—tables: *Clockwise, from top left,* two tablecloths, the top one a patchwork quilt; fabric stretched around tabletop and tacked on; local leaves under glass; needlepoint under glass.

Refinishing with paint: Decorative circles on these beds were stencilled
with spray paint. The color of the circles matches stripes.

ove left, make a fake marble top with
eral swirling colors. *Right*, highlight
ving with another color. *Below left*, a
in picnic table, hand-painted, becomes a
rk of art. The hanging light fixture was
de from beach glass. *Below right*, copy
esign from a fabric—bed, chest, and mir-
are painted with flowers like those on
tains and bedspread.

pencil, shoe polish, iodine crayon or touchup stick in a matching color. Wax and buff with paste wax like Simoniz or a silicone wax like Pledge; or lemon oil or boiled linseed oil, if this was original finish; or varnish.

A piece can be refinished several ways to show off or conceal the grain. Traditionally, it would be stripped to bare wood with a finish remover (a mess); then a stain would be rubbed on; then a wax, oil, or varnish added for protection. If the surface of a piece is smooth and clean, you may want to consider the easier alternative of covering the old finish rather than removing it. I have successfully applied a combination varnish stain in a matching color to revitalize an old finish, but the most common way of covering an old finish is with paint.

PAINTING

Remove old wax and dirt, and lightly sand a piece with sandpaper for better paint adhesion. Make sure it is dry.

Paint (this also applies to staining) in the following order:

Place a table or chair upside down with legs upright; work from inside the legs, the harder part to get to, to the outside. Turn piece upright, and paint the top or back and then the seat.

Place a chest or cabinet horizontally laid out. When painting a chest or cabinet, remove hardware and drawers and paint these separately. Paint the top, then lay down (the chest, not you), and paint the inside, sides, then the front and finally the legs.

Smaller pieces can be spray painted. To protect the surroundings, place in a carton or put lots of newspaper around. Try to spray paint outdoors on a dry day, when, ideally, all painting should be done, in an area protected from wind.

The easiest kind of paint to use and the one with its own built-in protective finish is high-gloss enamel. However, any kind of paint can be used on furniture as long as a washable finish is put over it. For example, a flat paint applied to walls could also be put on furniture to match, and when dry, the furniture covered with a coat of polyurethane varnish.

SPECIAL EFFECTS WITH PAINT

Antiquing kits: These consist basically of paint and a colored glaze that is applied to the paint finish with brush, paper towels, newspapers, etc., depending on the effect desired. Some kits do not include, but recommend applying, a clear finish; some are designed to create an imitation wood stain finish. To make your own glaze, mix a little oil color into a ready-made clear glaze mix or a mixture of linseed oil and turpentine. Antique kits are easy to use both because all (almost all—some kits omit sandpaper or brush) the ingredients are assembled for you and also because they are based on the failure-proof fact that the messier a mottled effect the better.

Painted designs: Easy to do; try a freehand design or simply paint each drawer of a chest a different color. Precise designs require more care. To paint stripes, apply masking tape to protect surrounding areas. Lift the tape off just before the paint hardens. Stencils should be held firmly in place by hand or by applying spray adhesive to the stencil. Stencils can be store-bought or homemade, cut from cardboard or improvised from cookie cutters, leaves, doilies, or whatever strikes the imagination. Any stiff bristle brush can be substituted for a stencil brush; for less precise lines, do not brush, but spray paint on.

Other special effects: Paste on paper cutouts from magazines, and protect with polyurethane. Attach stickers.

Glue on fabric or wallpaper, protect with polyurethane or cover with self-adhesive plastic. Instead of covering the entire piece, just do the drawers and top of a chest or the doors of a cabinet.

RE-COVERING CHAIRS AND COUCHES

Slip covering and reupholstering the traditional way is a complicated procedure to tackle, but there are several ways to get around it. Try to restore or change the color of the present fabric, or re-cover with new fabric in a casual way.

Spraying and Dyeing: Cover a faded vinyl or fabric with Fabspray (available in well-stocked hardware and variety stores) in a color similar to or darker than the present color. Follow the directions on the can. Dirt, discolorations, and patterns cannot be covered and will show through.

Cover small vinyl seats with latex enamel spray paint.

Paint an existing covering with acrylic paints, or decorate with permanent magic markers, or re-cover with canvas and then paint a "Picasso" on it.

If covering is easily removable, renew it by dyeing. Follow directions on the box or bottle. While dye is absorbed best when the hottest water available is used, if you are worried about shrinking use lukewarm water with twice the recommended amount of dye. A double quantity of dye should also be used in dyeing dark colors. Cotton dyes best, with acetate a close runner-up. Silk, rayon, nylon, and linen dye well; polyesters (which include Orlon and Dacron) do not and will dye only to a tint of the color. Fiber glass cannot be dyed.

Casual covering: Loosely cover large pieces, couches, and lounge chairs, with "fabric," including pretty sheets, blankets, or tablecloths. If the throw is too large and you do not want to cut, try tucking in and tucking under. To cut, lay fabric over furniture (optional tuck in and/or gather at sides with pins). Cut all excess material so that the cover just touches the floor, and fringe, or allow about two inches for a hem. Remove to hem and fringe. To attach permanently, gather fabric at corners and sew lightly to furniture.

Easiest Reupholstering

Slip seats: These seats of occasional or dining chairs literally slip off when the screws that hold the seats to the frames are removed. Either remove the old covering (if this can be done with ease) and use it as your pattern, or leave the old covering on and place the seat itself in the center of the wrong side of the fabric. Mark, roughly following the shape of the seat, adding on the necessary inches to allow for turning the fabric under the seat. Cut out fabric. Staple fabric to seat with high-compression stapler, pulling the fabric taut and stapling from the center of each side first and then working out to the corners. Cut off excess fabric at the corners and staple down. Incidentally, if you don't have a high-compression stapler, try a good-quality desk stapler that opens up into a tacking position.

To upholster a chair all over in a nonprofessional but often adequate way, lay fabric over each part of the chair, seat, back, arm, a piece at a time, and cut fabric to the size necessary to cover, allowing extra inches for mistakes. Attach fabric section by section with a staple gun or upholstery tacks. Trim away excess fabric with a very sharp single-edged razor blade. Glue (white glue) on a decorative gimp (trim) to cover staples, tacks, and mistakes.

Fabric Table Cover

This is a good way to cover an old table without refinishing, an electric cable spool, a stool or barrel with a round wood top nailed on. The tricky part is making a large circle with a string compass. Do this by tacking one end of a string to the approximate center of the fabric and chalk or crayon to the other end. Sew together more than one width of fabric, adding full or half widths to each side, to make a piece wide enough to cover the table down to the floor. To avoid piecing, use fabric 72 inches wide like felt or large sheets.

Wild wall coverings: One wall has a freehand painted design that extends onto the ceiling; another wall—and door—has magazine pictures pasted on, then varnished.

To calculate the width and length (this is the same in a circle) of fabric needed measure the table from the floor up, across the top of the table, and down the other side and add extra inches for seams or hem, if necessary. The length of the string will be one-half this measurement or the radius of the circle. Draw circle and cut. Glue or sew on a decorative trim to cover a raveled edge. Felt will not have to be fringed because it does not ravel.

If the table is going to be used for eating, place a small scarflike square of fabric or a cloth that can be lifted off and laundered over the table cover.

Paint and Wall Coverings

PAINTING WALLS

There are two kinds of paint: Alkyd oil-based paint that is solvent thinned with turpentine, and latex (acrylic) water-based paint that is thinned with water. Latex is generally considered the paint for the amateur to use, in part because cleaning up is easier. Finishes vary in degree of shine, and although different manufacturers have their own descriptive names for them, they are basically flat, semigloss, or high gloss. A glossy finish is sturdy and washable and can be used on all walls except those that are in poor condition because bumps and cracks will show up much more on a shiny wall than on a dull one.

All paint manufacturers make marvelous colors today, sold already mixed (stock colors) or custom mixed to your specifications. Stock colors are cheaper, and an unopened can usually may be returned. Small amounts of tinting colors, either oil- or water-based, can be added to change the color of a ready-mixed paint if the paint store does not carry a line of custom colors or if you do not want to pay the premium price.

Color charts available free from paint stores will give you an idea of the variety of color available. To preview how a color will look on a wall, try paint first in an inconspicuous spot. Wait until it dries. Or make a sample by painting a white card, drying it over a radiator and then taping it up to the wall.

It pays to buy the best paint and to buy enough of it. Not only is it frustrating to run out halfway through a job, but it is often impossible to buy more of *exactly* the same color. To assure uniformity of color when using more than one can of the same color, mix the contents of all the cans together before beginning. Buy enough rollers or brushes, the correct size and quality, plastic dropcloths to cover floors and furniture, and spackling compound for small cracks and holes that should be repaired before painting.

1. Put down plastic dropcloths and mounds of newspaper for protection.

2. Remove hardware and switchplates; loosen wall and ceiling fixtures, and cover with old cloths or newspaper.

3. Prepare walls. They should be as clean as possible, smooth and dry. Spackle cracks and holes; sand when dry.

Sand or scrape off old peeling paint. Seal bare spots with primer.

4. Paint in this order. Ceiling first. Paint with brush all around the perimeter; then fill in the ceiling with a roller on an extension stick, going across the narrowest part (width) of the ceiling.

Next, walls. First paint corners with a brush; then fill in with roller. To minimize dripping, the first stroke on the wall should go up. Then roll on paint in crisscross fashion. Do not stop painting in the middle of the ceiling or a wall. Now paint window frames and moldings.

To have full use of a staircase that is being painted, paint every other step and when dry paint the remaining ones.

Paint can be applied to almost any wall. Old wallpaper, even one with a texture, can be painted over as long as the paper is securely attached to the wall and any open seams or loose paper are sanded down. However, painted-over wallpaper cannot be removed, and a slight danger exists that the dye of a wallpaper will bleed or seams show through. If in doubt, test first.

While epoxy paint is normally recommended for ceramic tile walls, it is difficult to use. Try high-gloss enamel instead. For better adhesion, sand a very shiny tile first.

Save and label leftover paint. Do not store latex paint where it will freeze and consequently be ruined.

WALLPAPERING

Again make sure you have all necessary tools (available in a kit), the correct paste, and enough paper to complete the job. (See p. 220 for more information about wallpaper.)

1. Prepare walls. All walls, whether presently painted or papered, should be clean, dry, and smooth. Spackle holes and cracks, and sand rough spots. Smooth-surfaced old wallpaper can be left on if it is firmly attached to wall. Loose paper, tears, or open seams should be sanded down. Where

necessary, wallpaper can be removed by scraping, by steaming, and with wallpaper remover. Strippable wallpaper comes off very easily. Wash walls down with a solution of six parts water to one part ammonia. For better adhesion apply a coat of size especially to new and unpainted walls or newly plastered walls. For foil or vinyl use the proper glue, diluted, instead of size.

2. Remove hardware, fixtures, switch and outlet plates.

3. Now begin. Work on the floor or on a large table; dining or ping-pong tables are perfect. Trim selvage, if there is one. Measure the height of the wall area to be covered, add on a few inches for matching and mistakes, and cut. Put the first strip up on the right side as you go through the door. In this way the last strip, which is usually mismatched, will be inconspicuous over or behind the door.

4. To hang the first strip straight, establish a true vertical by dropping a plumb line. Hold a scissors tied to a long string from the ceiling. Mark the line where the string falls.

5. Paste about half the strip, then fold the pasted part toward the center of the strip. Do the same for the other half. Unfold top section, and align top and sides of strip on wall with plumb line, glue down, and smooth. Unfold other half, and smooth that down.

6. Apply first strip, pattern right side up, please, leaving a little extra paper at the top. If paper has a pattern, a complete repeat should be at the top. Trim excess at top and bottom. Attach other strips, matching pattern and butting (just touching) edges.

7. After a few minutes press seams with a seam roller.

8. Cover plates with paper and attach.

SELF-ADHESIVE PLASTIC (CON-TACT)

Easy to apply because you skip the glueing stage above. The plastic has so much "give" that it can go over surfaces not normally suited to papering, such as ceramic tile. No

Sheets, not only on the bed, but on walls, lampshade, and headboard. The pillowcase is trimmed with fringe.

special tools must be purchased. The back of a long comb can be used for smoothing. The manufacturer recommends that porous or unfinished surfaces, including raw wood, wallpaper, plaster, and wallboard, be covered first with a coat of shellac and allowed to dry for twenty-four hours.

Fabric Walls

The best fabric for walls is thin and tightly woven, like sheet material. For extra protection, it might have a stain-repellent finish, like Zepel. See p. 222 for how to estimate yardage.

Fabric can be put up several ways: with a high-compression staple gun (staples will go into sheetrock, wood, and some plaster walls), with tacks (harder to do), with double-faced tape (not as secure and the tape is expensive), or with white glue brushed first on nonporous walls (not on fabric). Combinations of one or more methods may be used.

The elegant but infinitely harder way to "upholster walls" is to attach thin strips of wood to the wall, put padding beneath, and tack fabric over onto the strips. Or you may "curtain walls" by sewing channels in top and bottom of fabric panel, then stretching and shirring over rods that are attached to the top and bottom of wall.

1. Follow instructions for applying wallpaper, Steps 2 to 8, omitting Steps 5 and 7.

2. Install according to method chosen (see above).

3. To hide seams and staples, glue on decorative trim or nail on thin wood molding.

Finishing Floors

Installing Wood, Resilient, or Carpet Tiles

Again make sure you have enough material (see p. 222 for

how much) and the proper tools. Buy self-adhesive tiles, which are extremely easy to install. The floor should be clean, dry, and smooth. When installing resilient tiles, a paper or plywood underlayment is sometimes necessary. (See p.169 "Resilient Floors.")

1. To find the center point of the floor, mark the center of each wall and draw a chalk or crayon line to the opposite wall. The center is the place where the two lines intersect. To reduce the amount of cutting, place a row of tiles on the floor along one line in each direction to the walls; then re-adjust center to allow for one full cut tile on two sides of the room. Note: The seams of new tiles should never be directly over the seams of the old ones below.

2. Attach according to instructions. Follow the grain or pattern of the tile. Tiles may have a direction arrow on the back.

3. Trim excess at walls with the cutting tool recommended for the type of tile being used.

Extra advice: Adhere leftover wood or resilient tiles to tops of furniture, chests, or tables to renew them; to walls to decorate them. Carpet squares make soft seat covers.

RENEWING OR REFINISHING WOOD FLOOR

Unless a new color or finish is desired, a beaten wood floor may not necessarily need to be completely refinished. First try a good cleaning with turpentine and steel wool. Or rent a heavy waxing machine that has steel wool pads on the bottom and wax floor, sweep up, then buff. Scratches can be covered with Old English Scratch Cover. Some wood stains can be applied right over an old finish to enrich or even it out. Holes should be filled in with wood filler. If a complete scraping and restaining is necessary, try to find a professional to do the job. Otherwise, rent the equipment—a large sanding machine and a smaller machine called an edger—from a hardware or floor-finishing store.

A painted floor, imitating tile laid in a diagonal harlequin design..

Buy sandpaper, wax, waxing pads, stain—and earplugs.

1. Keep the machine moving at all times to avoid gouging large and permanent holes in the floor. The edger will take care of areas the larger machine cannot reach and sandpaper will take care of the rest.

2. Clean floor after scraping and before staining or applying finishing coat.

3. The stripped floor can be left in its natural state or it can be stained any number of colors, including, red, blue,

black, green, white. Mix a little oil-based tinting color into a light natural stain to make your own colored stain. Finish floor with a penetrating sealer or varnish, such as polyurethane or wax (for advantages of each, see p.172).

PAINTING A FLOOR

Most clean, dry, smooth floors free of dirt and wax can be painted, including wood, concrete, and resilient (vinyl) floors (that have a minimum amount of traffic). The advantage of paint over stain is that the floor does not have to be scraped and that it is a one-step operation, unless two coats are needed, and can hide a badly discolored or ugly floor. (The disadvantage is that paint will chip; see p.173.) Put high-gloss enamel on wood floors or resilient floor covering; certain paints are specially formulated for use on concrete floors.

1. Sand down peeling paint, fill in holes with wood filler, and clean floor. Be sure to remove all wax, especially from a resilient floor, by washing first with turpentine or wax remover and then detergent.

2. Paint around perimeter with a brush; then fill in with a roller on an extension stick, starting in the farthest corner and working toward the door. When dry, cover with a second coat, if necessary.

3. On top of the base coat paint a free-hand design in other colors, or splatter colored paint by shaking a brushful of paint over the floor. Alternating squares of a parquet or tile floor can be painted another color, and a rug can be "painted on."

RESTORING RUGS AND CARPETS

1. The color of a rug can be renewed or changed to a darker color with dye or paint.

Spray a larger rug with Fabspray, but do this outdoors or

open the windows because the fumes are strong. Follow the other directions on the can.

A small rug can be dyed in a large basin or in a washing machine. Protect the inside of the machine by lining it first with aluminum foil. Follow the directions on the bottle or box.

Spray paint can recolor rugs, but it leaves a gummy sticky surface on most rugs with a pile. However, it works well with sisal or grass rugs. The neatest way to spray a rug is to hang the rug outside on a clothesline or fence. Protect the surrounding area, if possible. One way around this is to paint the rug the same color as the area, green! Several coats may be necessary. If the rug is painted on the floor, lay large amounts of newspaper beneath it.

2. Add new fringe; sew or glue it on with fabric glue.

3. To make a new rug, sew together many rug samples or glue the samples to a heavy piece of canvas.

4. Decorate a heavy piece of canvas with acrylic paint.

Window Shades and Curtains

How to Make or Cover a Window Shade

An old shade can be renewed by covering it with fabric, wallpaper, or self-adhesive plastic; by trimming it with fringe, ribbon, colored tape, stickers, fabric cutouts; by decorating it with acrylic paint or permanent markers. A shade can be made by attaching fabric to a roller or glueing the fabric onto shade cloth. Fabric should be thin and tightly woven, like a sheet. To find out how much fabric is needed, either measure or use the old shade cloth as a pattern. Or measure the window, first the width from point to point inside or on the frame, adding on 2 inches for side hems or overlap, then the length from the location of the roller to the windowsill, adding on 18 inches for rollup and slat pocket. One width of fabric is usually wide enough. Try to avoid seaming; buy a wider fabric instead.

1. Method One. Buy a window shade kit that comes complete with special self-laminating shade cloth. Made very easy, but at a price.

2. Method Two. First test compatibility of shade cloth and glue in a small area. Spray adhesive* onto either an old or new shade that is being covered and put white glue along the edges. Carefully place fabric or wallpaper that has been cut to size on the shade cloth. Smooth down. Turn under excess fabric on sides and glue. Wallpaper works best on a shade that is not subject to a great deal of rolling up and down. Self-adhesive plastic can also be applied in this way.

3. Method Three. Staple or tack measured and cut piece of fabric, heavy wallpaper (vinyl works well), or self-adhesive plastic (with the backing left *on*) to an old or new roller. To roll properly, material must be cut straight and stapled squarely along guideline on roller.

4. Method Four. Paint or spray paint a shade that stays stationary; movement will crack paint.

Glue slat to shade bottom or put through a fabric easing (hem at bottom). Attach a shade pull.

How to Make Curtains

Follow the instructions for measuring and calculating the amount of fabric on p.224,"How Much Material."

1. Cut panels of fabric so that a full repeat, if there is a pattern, will be at the top of a long curtain or the bottom of a short curtain. Add about 8 inches for hems and heading.

2. If more than one width of fabric is necessary, sew panels of fabric together. Put right sides together, matching the pattern; then stitch and press flat. If window is narrow or fabric is wide, it may not be necessary to sew panels of fabric together at all. For example, if a window is 36 inches wide, a pair of curtains of double fullness can be made from

---

* Hard to find but worth the search. The best spray adhesive is one made to hold fabric to fabric. If necessary, substitute diluted white glue brushed on.

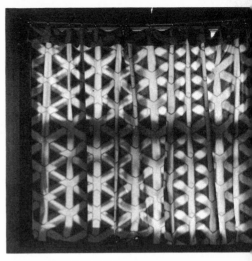

At left, home-sewn curtains made by following a pattern in *Simplicity's Home Decorator* series, which also includes bedspreads, shower curtains, and tablecloths. *Below*, no-sew curtain and bedspread—pillowcases turned over and clipped, and a fitted sheet over, not under, the bedding. Detail of curtains is shown directly above.

Assorted accessories: *Opposite*, *top*, attractively arranged, they dress up a dull radiator. *Below*, a camel bag catchall saves steps up and down stairs. *On this page*, *top*, a decorative and functional fan. *Below left*, to fill an unused fireplace, a painting on a stand. *Below*, *right*, a pretty planter box (to use for cut flowers, put a jar in the box or basket to hold water).

Just for fun: paint a scale; cover a bead
wagon in self-adhesive plastic; paint a
old toilet seat (a potential planter?).

rking with mirrors: *Top* surround a mirror with sea- s. *Right*, decorate a medi- cabinet with plastic coasters colored tape. *Below*, embel- a mirror with a painted de-

two 36-inch-wide panels of fabric; two 48-inch-wide panels of fabric will make a pair of almost triple fullness. Hem raw edges on the bottom and, if necessary, on the sides.

2. The heading or top of the curtain must be finished, gathered, or pleated or hardware attached to it. The easiest way to make a pleated top is to sew on straight or scalloped pleated tape. Then insert special hooks that both "pleat" the fabric and hold the curtain to the rod. Or sew a narrow channel on top and shir the fabric onto the rod. Sew loops of fabric or sew on a tape that has loops already attached to it. Sew on rings or buy the kind that just clip on without sewing.

3. No-sew curtains can be made from sheets which already have finished ends, if the sheet is roughly the same length as the window area to be covered. Cut a slit in one hemmed end to slip a curtain rod through or attach clip-on rings to sheet or pillowcase (for café curtains). If the sheet is too long, fold over excess material at top before clipping.

Extra advice: The easiest-to-install rod is a spring-tension curtain rod. No nails, screws, or work required.

Potpourri

—Make your own fabrics. On plain white or light-colored sheets dye or tie dye, paint with acrylic, or draw with permanent magic markers.

—Customize bedspreads by trimming them with ribbon, colored iron-on tape, appliqués, and fringe.

—Create floor cushions by folding 2 yards of 36-inch-wide fabric in half, right side facing in, stitching three sides, turning it right side out and filling with approximately 8- to 12-pound bags of shredded polyurethane foam.

—Decorate and rejuvenate accessories—picture frames, mirrors, wastebaskets, tissue boxes, lamps and lampshades—with scraps of fabric, wallpaper, self-adhesive plastic; with trimmings; or with paint.

THE COUNTRY
HOMEOWNER'S
BOOKSHELF

ARTHUR, ERIC, and WHITNEY, DUDLEY, *The Barn.* Greenwich, Conn., New York Graphic Society, 1972.

BERGEN, JOHN, *All About Upholstery.* New York, Hawthorn, 1962.

BERGER, ROBERT, *All About Antiquing and Restoring Furniture.* New York, Hawthorn, 1971.

COBB, HUBBARD, *How to Paint Anything.* New York, Macmillan, 1972.

FISHER, KAREN, *Living for Today.* New York, The Viking Press, 1972.

GLADSTONE, BERNARD, *New York Times Complete Manual of Home Repair.* New York, Macmillan, 1956.

HIGSON, JAMES, *The Higson Home Builder.* Los Angeles, Calif., Nash, 1972.

HORNUNG, CLARENCE P., *Treasury of American Design.* New York, Harry N. Abrams, 1972. 2 vols.

House and Garden's Complete Guide to Interior Decoration. New York, Simon and Schuster, 1970.

KINNEY, RALPH PARSONS, *The Complete Book of Furniture Repair and Refinishing,* rev. ed. New York, Scribners, 1971.

249

Manual of Home Repairs, Remodeling and Maintenance. New York, Grosset & Dunlap, 1969.

ORMSBEE, THOMAS FIELD, *Guide to Early American Furniture.* New York, Bantam Books, 1971.

Reader's Digest Practical Guide to Home Landscaping. Pleasantville, N.Y., Reader's Digest Associates, 1972.

Sunset Book of Carpentry. Menlo Park, Calif., Lane Books, 1972.

Sunset Books Furniture Upholstery and Repair. Menlo Park, Calif., Lane Books, 1970.

Sunset Books Remodeling Your Home. Menlo Park, Calif., Lane Books, 1958.

Sunset Books, *Basic Carpentry Illustrated.* Menlo Park, Calif., Lane Books, 1972.

INDEX

252

Credits

Unless indicated otherwise, photographs were taken by the author, and names given are owners of the homes. Pictures taken by Sandra Roome are indicated by "(SR)."
p. 8 Copyright 1972 Downe Publishing Inc. Reprinted by permission of *American Home*, p. 14 Sally and Charles Bates (sign), Mr. and Mrs. Henry Kibel (door), Hazel Skidmore (blackboard), Dr. and Mrs. Jordan Brown (bells), p. 16 Mr. and Mrs. R. A. Aurthur, p. 17 Kibel, p. 27 Aletha Haley, p. 30 Gay Mclean, designer (bold design), p. 31 Mr. and Mrs. Edward McDonough (treads), Arthur Rosenstein (eclectic), Clifford Stanton, designer (lavabo), p. 42 Sandra Roome (SR), p. 45 Dr. and Mrs. Richard Gibbs (matching), McDonough (painted tub), p. 46 Jeanne Campbell (SR) (piggyback), p. 48 Jeanne Campbell (SR) (self-adhesive); Saralee and Mike Singer (antique accessories), p. 49 Jeanna Carr, designer (SR), p. 50 James Trees (Garland), p. 52 Lundquist & Stonehill, architects (work/eating area); Kibel (bentwood chairs); Mr. and Mrs. Fredric Varady (banquette), p. 53 Giggs (three lights); William D. Helburn (butcher block), p. 58 Shirley L. Kauffman, L. Dees-Porch, designer (above); Adele Applebaum (below), p. 60 Mr. and Mrs. Wm. McGrail, p. 62 Robert A. M. Stern and John Hagmann, architects photo: Wm. Maris, Reprinted from *House Beautiful* August, 1972, Copyright The Hearst Corporation, 1972, p. 63 Kauffman, W. M. Wehle, designer, p. 64 Lundquist & Stonehill, architects, p. 65 Rosenstein (tub) Mr. and Mrs. Harold Cooper, p. 66 Philip Landeck (SR), p. 68 Carr (SR), p. 73 John and Sally Veronis, p. 74 Applebaum (corner), p. 75 Mr. and Mrs. B. O. Siler (six); Gerda Clark, Abraham & Straus Home, Fashions Coordinator (ceiling); Aurthur (king); Mr. and Mrs. Ted Deglin (drawer), p. 78 Helburn, p. 79 Kibel (bed); Cooper (two closets); Stanton (corner cabinet), p. 81 Gibbs, p. 82 Trudi and Speed Vogel (fishing rod), p. 84 Rosenstein (island); Mr. and Mrs. Tom Mohr (cabinets), p. 85 Gibbs, p. 86 Stanton (grocery cabinet), p. 87 Applebaum (low shelf); Campbell (SR) (laundry), p. 88 Photo: Jon Naar, p. 90 Stern & Hagmann, architects; photo: Wm. Maris Reprinted from *House Beautiful*, August 1972, Copyright, The Hearst Corporation 1972 (pool house); Lois and Dr. Robert Gould (pillows), p. 91 Cooper, p. 93 Lundquist & Stonehill, p. 94 Stanton (french), p. 95 Mr. and Ms. Lawrence Stoll (Palm Beach); Camp Red Wing for Girls (wicker), p. 97 Kauffman, p. 98 Deglin, p. 102 Jody and Max Schneier, p. 103 Jay Spectre (plexiglass), Helburn (roulette), p. 105 Stern photo: John Hill, p. 107 Roome (SR), p. 109 Stanton, p. 111 Cooper (sheets); photo: Jon Naar (stall), p. 114 Haley (bookcase), p. 115 McGrail (sled); Varady (tiles), p. 119 Helburn, p. 122 Mike and Saralee Singer (cage); Speed & Trudi Vogel (vinyl); Siler (milkman), p. 123 Varady (tray); Aurthur (barrell); Kibel (marble), p. 130 Rosenstein-Carr (SR), p. 134 Mr. and Mrs. Robert Geniesse (flag); Stoll (scallops), p. 137 Zajac & Callahan (SR), p. 140 Stoll (above); Rosenstein-Carr, (below), p. 144 Horace Gifford, designer, p. 146 Mr. and Mrs. Jack Maurer (shutters); Siler (frame), p. 149 Schneier (tiebacks); Stanton (shade), p. 150 Aurthur (matchstick); Vogel (cafés); Helburn (tiebacks), p. 152 Lundquist & Stonehill (blinds); Cooper (shutters); Bates (SR) (awning), p. 155 Maurer, Gretchen Van Tassel, artist, p. 157 Vogel (sisal); Cooper (tile); Helburn (brick), p. 158 Gay McLean, designer (one wall); Bates (SR) (redpaint), Maurer (panels), p. 159 Brown (cork); Shirley Bakal (cabinets); Mr. and Mrs. Warren Benedek (checks), p. 160 Mr. and Mrs. Robert Haag-Phyllis Horton, designer, p. 162 Siler (blankets); Zajac & Callahan (SR), p. 165 Stanton (border), p. 173 McDonough, p. 174 Zajac & Callahan (SR), p. 178 Geniesse (park bench); Bates (SR) (Sisal), p. 179 Kibel, p. 180 Bates (SR) (gazebo); Stoll (Florida), p. 181 Spectre, p. 187 Kibel (hanging), Edith & Norman Zelenko (Strandkorb), p. 190 Haley (cement); Kibel (flues), p. 191 McGrail, p. 197 Deglin (waterfall), p. 198 McGrail (driftwood), p. 199 Sculpture by Menashe Kadishman, p. 202 Gibbs (metal); Cooper (pit), p. 203 Kibel (header); Gould (stretcher); Stanton (herringbone), p. 204 Mohr (paper lamp); Siler (floor light), p. 205 Stanton (keg); photo: Carol Eisner (tennis), p. 206 Haley (dry); Carr (SR) (cabinet); Stanton (armoire), p. 207 Gibbs (stove); Betty Rollin and Arthur Herzog (wagon), p. 208 Helburn (niche); Maurer, Clyde Rich, designer (wallpaper); Spectre (plexiglass), p. 210 Norman Jaffe, architect (exterior view of house on jacket), Hal McKusick, photographer, p. 216 Red Wing, p. 218 Harold Cooper (scraps); Dr. Richard Gibbs (driftwood), p. 221 Kibel (kites); McGrail (horsecollar), p. 223 Varady, p. 225 Brown (patchwork); Red Wing (fabric); Haley (leaves), p. 226 Haag-Horton, p. 227 Wayne (flowers); Cooper (marble); Haag-Horton (carving), p. 232 Siler, p. 236 Singer, p. 243 Simplicity Patterns, Siler (no-sew), p. 246 Vogel (scale) p. 244 Applebaum (camel), p. 245 Gibbs (fan), Special thanks to Arnold Skolnick, Lari Siler and Igor Bakht for their help and to Thomas Pizzillo & Sons for the information on upholstery and slipcover yardage requirements on pages 222 and 224.